Also by Stanley Kunitz

Intellectual Things *(poems)*

Passport to the War *(poems)*

Selected Poems 1928–1958

Poems of John Keats *(editor)*

The Testing-Tree *(poems)*

Poems of Akhmatova *(translator, with Max Hayward)*

Story under Full Sail, by Andrei Voznesensky *(translator)*

The Coat without a Seam *(poems: limited edition)*

The Terrible Threshold *(English edition only)*

A Kind of Order, A Kind of Folly: Essays & Conversations

Orchard Lamps, by Ivan Drach *(editor and co-translator)*

The Poems of
STANLEY KUNITZ

1928-1978

The Poems of
STANLEY KUNITZ

1928-1978

———

An Atlantic Monthly Press Book

Little, Brown and Company — Boston–Toronto

Second Printing

LIBRARY OF CONGRESS CATALOGING IN PUBLICATION DATA

Kunitz, Stanley Jasspon, 1905–
   The poems of Stanley Kunitz, 1928–1978.
   "An Atlantic Monthly Press book."
   Includes index.
   I. Title.
PS3521.U7P6   811'.5'2   79-463
ISBN 0-316-50711-3
ISBN 0-316-50710-5 pbk.

The poems in "The Layers: New Poems" have been previously published in: *American Poetry Review* ("The Layers"), *Antaeus* ("Quinnapoxet"), *The Atlantic* ("What of the Night?" "The Catch," "The Quarrel," "The Unquiet Ones," and "My Sisters"), *Craft Horizons* of the American Craft Council ("Words for the Unknown Makers: An American Suite"), *Iowa Review* ("Firesticks"), *Malahat Review* ("Meditations on Death [Ungaretti]" under the title "Death Thoughts"), *New England Review* ("Route Six" and "Silence"), *The New Yorker* ("Signs and Portents" and "The Lincoln Relics"), *Salmagundi* ("The Knot"), and *The Nation* ("The Crystal Cage," also in *A Joseph Cornell Album* by Dore Ashton).

ATLANTIC–LITTLE, BROWN BOOKS
ARE PUBLISHED BY
LITTLE, BROWN AND COMPANY
IN ASSOCIATION WITH
THE ATLANTIC MONTHLY PRESS

MV

Designed by Susan Windheim

*Published simultaneously in Canada
by Little, Brown & Company (Canada) Limited*

PRINTED IN THE UNITED STATES OF AMERICA

To
    Elise
    Gretchen
    Babette
        the nearest of my tribe

Author's Note

Twenty years ago, when I was preparing the manuscript of my
Selected Poems 1928–1958, I thought it important to arrange the
contents in groups that bore some relevance to the themes, the
arguments, that had preoccupied my imagination since I began
writing seriously for publication. This served a purpose, but led
to some confusion as to the dating of my poems, among those
who care about such matters. The present volume, summing
up my fifty years of poetry — a stupefying calculation! — is
arranged chronologically, though in reverse order, beginning
with new poems and stepping back to my start. As one who
was not predestined, either by nature or by art, to become a
prolific poet, I must admit it pleases me that, thanks to longev-
ity, the body of my work is beginning to acquire a bit of heft.
A few poems — not much more than a handful — have been
omitted from this collection, simply because I could not bear
the sight of them again. I have tinkered here and there with
some of my early poems, but have not tried to revise them
radically in order to satisfy the dictates of a later style. In recent
years I have worked extensively with translations, particularly
from the Russian, of which I have made room for only a modest
sampling. Where I felt I could say something pertinent about
the occasions, allusions, or sources of poems, I have supplied
a few unsystematic notes in an appendix, which can be safely
ignored by most readers.

S. K.

Contents

THE LAYERS: NEW POEMS

The Knot	1
What of the Night?	2
Quinnapoxet	4
Silence (Akhmadulina)	6
Words for the Unknown Makers: A Garland of Commemorative Verses	
To a Slave Named Job	8
Sacred to the Memory	9
Girl With Sampler	10
Trompe l'Oeil	11
A Blessing of Women	12
The Catch	15
The Crystal Cage	16
Signs and Portents	18
Firesticks	21
The Lincoln Relics	22
Meditations on Death (Ungaretti)	26
The Quarrel	30

The Unquiet Ones   31
My Sisters   32
Route Six   33
The Layers   35

THE TESTING-TREE   1971

Journal for My Daughter   39
The Illumination   45
Three Floors   47
The Flight of Apollo   48
Around Pastor Bonhoeffer   49
King of the River   52
The Mulch   55
Robin Redbreast   56
Indian Summer at Land's End   58
Summer Solstice (Mandelstam)   59
Tristia (Mandelstam)   60
After the Last Dynasty   62
River Road   64
The Magic Curtain   66
The System   69
Hand-rolled Cigarettes (Yevtushenko)   70
The Customs Collector's Report   72
The Gladiators   74
Bolsheviks (Stolzenberg)   76
The Mound Builders   77
Boris Pasternak (Akhmatova)   80

Dante (Akhmatova)   82

Cleopatra (Akhmatova)   83

The Artist   84

The Bottom of the Glass   85

The Portrait   86

An Old Cracked Tune   87

Again! Again!   88

The Testing-Tree   89

The Game   93

THIS GARLAND, DANGER *from* SELECTED POEMS
1928–1958   1958

The Science of the Night   97

Green Ways   99

When the Light Falls   100

Among the Gods   101

As Flowers Are   102

The Waltzer in the House   103

Sotto Voce   104

Grammar Lesson   105

She Wept, She Railed   107

Foreign Affairs   108

The Unwithered Garland   110

The Man Upstairs   111

The Approach to Thebes   112

The Dark and the Fair   114

The Thief   116

End of Summer   119

Goose Pond   120

The Dragonfly   122

The War Against the Trees   125

The Thing That Eats the Heart   127

By Lamplight   128

The Scourge   129

Off Point Lotus   130

Rover   131

Hermetic Poem   132

To the Reader (Baudelaire)   133

The Way Down   135

The Class Will Come to Order   138

The Summing-Up   140

A Choice of Weapons   141

Revolving Meditation   143

A Spark of Laurel   146

from PASSPORT TO THE WAR   1944

Reflection by a Mailbox   151

My Surgeons   153

The Tutored Child   155

The Signal from the House   156

Father and Son   157

Welcome the Wrath   159

Night Letter   160

The Last Picnic   162

The Hemorrhage 163

The Harsh Judgment 165

Confidential Instructions 166

The Economist's Song 167

The Old Clothes Man 168

Careless Love 170

The Supper Before Last 171

The Daughters of the Horseleech 172

Between the Acts 173

This Day This World 174

The Illusionist 175

Invocation 176

No Word 177

The Last Question 178

How Long Is the Night? 179

The Guilty Man 180

The Fitting of the Mask 181

The Reckoning 183

Open the Gates 184

from INTELLECTUAL THINGS 1930

Change 187

Geometry of Moods 188

For the Word Is Flesh 190

Twilight 192

Single Vision 193

Particular Lullaby 195

Promise Me   196
Strange Calendar   197
Poem   198
Deciduous Branch   200
The Words of the Preacher   201
Mens Creatrix   202
Ambergris   203
Approach of Autumn   204
The Pivot   205
He   206
Very Tree   207
Prophecy on Lethe   209
Postscript   210
Lovers Relentlessly   212
Death in Moonlight   214
Regard of Tangents   215
For Proserpine   216
When the Dead Arise   218
Parting   219
I Dreamed That I Was Old   220
Night-Piece   221
Me and the Rock   222
Transformations   223
First Love   224
Last Words   225
Eagle   226
Motion of Wish   227
So Intricately Is This World Resolved   228

Benediction   229

The Separation   231

In a Strange House   232

Master and Mistress   233

Organic Bloom   234

Beyond Reason   235

Vita Nuova   236

                Notes and Index

Notes   239

Index   245

THE LAYERS

—

New Poems

THE KNOT

I've tried to seal it in,
that cross-grained knot
on the opposite wall,
scored in the lintel of my door,
but it keeps bleeding through
into the world we share.
Mornings when I wake,
curled in my web,
I hear it come
with a rush of resin
out of the trauma
of its lopping-off.
Obstinate bud,
sticky with life,
mad for the rain again,
it racks itself with shoots
that crackle overhead,
dividing as they grow.
Let be! Let be!
I shake my wings
and fly into its boughs.

WHAT OF THE NIGHT?

I

One summer, like a stone
dropped down a well,
I sank into myself
and raked
the bottom slime.
When I stretched out my thigh
it touched the dark,
and the dark rolled over me.
A brackish life
filled the cups of my skin.
Then gradually I heard
above the steady
breathing of the land
a high, inhuman chord
light-years away,
out of a cleaner space,
a more innocent age,
as when pilot angels
with crystal eyes and streaming hair
rode planets through the skies,
and each one sang
a single ravishing note
that melted
into the music of the spheres.

What wakes me now
like the country doctor
startled in his sleep?
Why does my racing heart
shuffle down the hall
for the hundredth time
to answer the night-bell?
Whoever summons me has need of me.
How could I afford
to disobey that call?
A gentle, insistent ring
pulled me from my bed,
from loving arms,
though I know
I am not ready yet
and nobody stands on the stoop,
not even a stray cat
slouches under the sodium lamp.
Deceived! or self-deceived.
I can never atone for it.
Oh I should be the one
to swell the night with my alarm!
When the messenger comes again
I shall pretend
in a childish voice
my father is not home.

QUINNAPOXET

I was fishing in the abandoned reservoir
back in Quinnapoxet,
where the snapping turtles cruised
and the bullheads swayed
in their bower of tree-stumps,
sleek as eels and pigeon-fat.
One of them gashed my thumb
with a flick of his razor fin
when I yanked the barb
out of his gullet.
The sun hung its terrible coals
over Buteau's farm: I saw
the treetops seething.

They came suddenly into view
on the Indian road,
evenly stepping
past the apple orchard,
commingling with the dust
they raised, their cloud of being,
against the dripping light
looming larger and bolder.
She was wearing a mourning bonnet
and a wrap of shining taffeta.
"Why don't you write?" she cried
from the folds of her veil.

"We never hear from you."
I had nothing to say to her.
But for him who walked behind her
in his dark worsted suit,
with his face averted
as if to hide a scald,
deep in his other life,
I touched my forehead
with my swollen thumb
and splayed my fingers out —
in deaf-mute country
the sign for father.

SILENCE

—from Bella Akhmadulina

Just who was so powerful and clever?
Who took my voice away, out of my throat?
The black wound in my throat
doesn't know how to cry about it.

Dear March, how much I want to sing
your simple deeds;
but the nightingales of my words are dead
and now their gardens are dictionaries.

Snowfall, shrubbery, hillside
implore me, "Celebrate us in song!"
But muteness shapes an O
like vapor in my mouth.

What's inspiration but pure breath,
the soul sucking the moment in?
Another breath won't save me
unless I speak the word.

I gasp and puff and falsify,
so that I won't remain in debt

to the beauty of trees in the snow,
which I am dumb to praise.

Let me ease my swollen pulse,
by accident or any way at all, until
I reel with the bright gush of song,
until I become a poem learned by heart.

And because I was so mute
and loved the names of all the words
and suddenly am tired unto death
please help me, everyone, sing me alive.

WORDS FOR THE UNKNOWN MAKERS
A Garland of Commemorative Verses*

TO A SLAVE NAMED JOB

Dreaming of Africa
and the kings of the dark land,
bearer of a suffering name,
you carved this Indian
out of a man-sized log
to be your surrogate
and avatar.
Outside the smoke-shop
he stands aloof and bold,
with his raised foot poised
for the oppressor's neck.
The cigars he offers
are not for sale.
They fit his hand
as though they were a gun.

* On the occasion of the exhibition "The Flowering of American Folk Art," at the Whitney Museum in 1974. See Note on p. 239.

SACRED TO THE MEMORY

Mourn for Polly Botsford, aged thirty-nine,
and for her blossom Polly, one year old,
and for Gideon, her infant son, nipped in the bud.
And mourn for the mourners under the graveside willow,
trailing its branches of inverted V's,
those women propped like bookends on either side of the
    tomb,
and that brace of innocents in matching calico
linked to their mother's grief with a zigzag clasp of hands,
as proper in their place as stepping-stones.
Mourn, too, for the nameless painter of the scene
who, like them all, was born to walk a while
beside the brook whose source is common tears,
till suddenly it's time to unlatch the narrow gate
and pass through the church that is not made with walls
and seek another home, a different sky.

GIRL WITH SAMPLER
"A Soft Answer Turneth Away Wrath"

She sat by the window,
lips pursed, plying her needle.
The parlor wall waited
for a family showpiece.
"Do it right, child!" said her mother.
This way she learned the ABC's,
improved her mind with Bible verses,
embroidered her name into her dowry:
Nabby Dexter of Providence, Rhode Island,
Patricia Goodeshall, Abigail Fleetwood,
Elizabeth Finney, virtuoso of stitches
(cross . . . flat . . . buttonhole . . .
satin . . . outline . . . bullion knot).
Some prized the task and its performance,
others groaned as they ripped out blunders
in and around the moral sentences.
One of them added a line to her sampler:
"And Hated every bit of it."

TROMPE L'OEIL

Whoever made this piece began
with boards of honest country pine
fit for a modest sideboard table.
As for the finishing,
I doubt he had a plan,
he simply led his brushes on,
or maybe it was they that led,
stippling and graining,
simulating to a T
maple, walnut, birch,
imitating inlays and veneers,
putting on the airs of Sheraton.
Utility took fantasy for wife.
O lucky day!
The fun was in the afterplay
when the true artisan
tells his white lies.

A BLESSING OF WOMEN

"Remember me is all I ask,
And, if remembered be a task,
Forget me."
      — Album verses by Minerva Butler Miller,
        tinsmith's daughter, peddler's wife, c. 1850

BLESS ZERUAH HIGLEY GUERNSEY of Castleton, Vermont, who sheared the wool from her father's sheep; washed, carded, and spun it into yarn; steeped it in dyes concocted from native berries, barks, and plants; and embroidered it, in Double Kensington chain stitch, on a ground of homespun squares until they bloomed with fruit, shells, snow crystals, flowers, and cats, most singularly a noble blue cat; each of the eighty-odd panels being different from the rest, and the whole , a paragon of American needlework design, executed in the ardor of her long pre-nuptial flight, and accomplished in 1835 for her ill-starred wedding day.

BLESS DEBORAH GOLDSMITH, genteel itinerant, who supported her aged and impoverished parents by traveling from house to house in the environs of Hamilton, New York, painting portraits of the families who gave her bed and board, until she limned in watercolors the likeness of one George Throop, who married her, therewith terminating her travels and leading to her premature decease, at twenty-seven.

BLESS MRS. AUSTIN ERNEST of Paris, Illinois, whose husband, a local politician of no other fame, organized in 1853 a rally for the Presidential candidate of the new Republican party, following which she gathered the material used to decorate the stand wherefrom the immortal Lincoln spoke and, with scissors and needle and reverential heart, transformed it into a quilted patchwork treasure.

BLESS MARY ANN WILLSON, who in 1810 appeared in the frontier town of Greenville, New York, with her "romantic attachment," a Miss Brundage, with whom she settled in a log cabin, sharing their lives and their gifts, Miss Brundage farming the land, Miss Willson painting dramatic scenes with a bold hand, in colors derived from berries, brickdust, and store paint, and offering her compositions for sale as "rare and unique works of art."

BLESS HANNAH COHOON, who dwelt in the Shaker "City of Peace," Hancock, Massachusetts, where a spirit visited her, as frequently happened there, and gave her "a draft of a beautiful Tree pencil'd on a large sheet of white paper," which she copied out, not knowing till later, with assistance from the Beyond, that it was the Tree of Life; and who saw in another vision, which she likewise reproduced, the Elders of the community feasting on cakes at a table beneath mulberry trees; and who believed, according to the faith of the followers of Mother Ann Lee, that Christ would return to earth in female form.

BLESS IN A CONGREGATION, because they are so numerous, those industrious schoolgirls stitching their alphabets; and the deft ones with needles at lacework, crewel, knitting; and mistresses of spinning, weaving, dyeing; and daughters of tinsmiths painting their ornamental mottoes; and hoarders of rags hooking and braiding their rugs; and adepts in cutouts, valentines, stencils, still lifes, and "fancy pieces"; and middle-aged housewives painting, for the joy of it, landscapes and portraits; and makers of bedcovers with names that sing in the

13

night — Rose of Sharon, Princess Feather, Delectable Mountains, Turkey Tracks, Drunkard's Path, Indiana Puzzle, Broken Dishes, Star of LeMoyne, Currants and Coxcomb, Rocky-Road-to-Kansas.

BLESS THEM AND GREET THEM as they pass from their long obscurity, through the gate that separates us from our history, a moving rainbow-cloud of witnesses in a rising hubbub, jubilantly turning to greet one another, this tumult of sisters.

THE CATCH

It darted across the pond
toward our sunset perch,
weaving in, up, and around
a spindle of air,
this delicate engine
fired by impulse and glitter,
swift darning-needle,
gossamer dragon,
less image than thought,
and the thought come alive.
Swoosh went the net
with a practiced hand.
"Da–da, may I look too?"
You may look, child,
all you want.
This prize belongs to no one.
But you will pay all
your life for the privilege,
all your life.

THE CRYSTAL CAGE

for Joseph Cornell

To climb the belltower,
step after step,
in the grainy light,
without breathing harder;
to spy on each landing
a basket of gifts,
a snowbox of wonders:
pressed flowers, pieces
of colored glass,
a postcard from Niagara Falls,
agates, cut-outs of birds,
and dozing in the pile,
in faded mezzotint,
Child Mozart at the Clavichord.
Three days you fasted
to bring you angels;
your square-toed shoes,
friends of your plodding,
are turning weightless.
When the pear-shaped, brindled cat
who lives under the belfry
jumps into your arms
you are not surprised
by the love-look in her amber eyes,

or by the blissful secrets
she confides to you
in oval, pellucid tones.
What if the iron overhead
suddenly starts pounding?
What if, outside,
a terrible storm is raging?
What if, below,
your twisted brother is calling?

SIGNS AND PORTENTS

1

Jonathan, the last of the giant tortoises
on wind-beaten Saint Helena,
misses his island mate,
who died in a fall from a cliff
a century ago.
He is ancient and crusty,
more lonely than Bonaparte
strutting on the volcanic beach,
reviewing his triumphs.
Lately he has made himself
a deliberate nuisance
to the sporting set
of the British Crown Colony
by butting and upending benches
near the tennis courts
and disrupting croquet games
by sitting on the croquet balls.

2

At the Porch of the Caryatids
on the Acropolis
the noble supportive maidens
are stepping down

from their weathered pedestals,
one by one,
to seek asylum in a museum.
Their places will be taken
by identical synthetic sisters
conditioned to withstand
the high, classic, polluted air.

3

Three thousand years ago
they soaked him in pickling brine,
stuffed his body with resins,
baked him in desert heat.
He was Ramses the Second,
feared by Hittites and Israelites,
the hard Pharaoh of *Exodus,*
colossal as the temples
his minions sweated out of rock.
Paris has him now
on temporary loan.
In the aseptic laboratory
of the Musée de l'Homme,
where he lies in state
for special treatment,
who will cure the old mummy
of the loathsome fire
raging under his bandages?

4

Children at play in a field,
tumbling down a hole
into the pristine Palaeolithic,
showed us the way,

ripped the lid from the grotto.
We sped to the spot on wheels
with our cameras and basket lunches.
Now the bison of Lascaux,
prodded from their centuries
of limestone sleep, are sick.
Clots of a virulent mold
suppurate on their flanks,
emitting a green stain.
We name it *la maladie verte,*
an infection from people.
At the back of our minds
squat figures, whose hairy hands
carried torches and the dream of art
through cheerless labyrinths,
gabble in the shadows.

5

On Twelfth Street in Manhattan,
opposite St. Vincent's Mental Pavilion,
while I was sweeping the sidewalk
of its increment of filth,
deposited by dogs and unleashed humans,
a blue van rolled by
with its sidepanel reading:
WORLD FINISHING AND DYEING COMPANY.
I did not catch the face of the driver.

FIRESTICKS

Conjugations of the verb "to be"
asleep since Adam's fall
wake from bad phosphor dreams
heavy with mineral desire.
Earthstruck they leave
their ferny prints of spines
in beds of stone
and carry private moons
down history's long roads,
gaudy with flags.
The one they walk behind
who's named "I AM"
they chose with spurts of flame
to guide them
like the pillar of a cloud
into the mind's white exile.

THE LINCOLN RELICS

"*A Lincoln exhibit on view in the Great Hall makes the 16th President of the United States, born 167 years ago, seem very real. Displayed are the contents of his pockets the night he was assassinated, a miniature portrait never before exhibited, and two great documents from the Library's collections, the Gettysburg Address and the Second Inaugural Address.*"

— Library of Congress Information Bulletin,
February 1976

I

Cold-eyed, in Naples once,
while the congregation swooned,
I watched the liquefaction
of a vial of precious blood,
and wondered only
how the trick was done.
Saint's bones are only bones
to me, but here,
where the stage is set
without a trace of gore,
these relics on display —
watchfob and ivory pocket knife,
a handkerchief of Irish linen,
a button severed from his sleeve —
make a noble, dissolving music
out of homely fife and drum,
and that's miraculous.

His innocence was to trust
the better angels of our nature,
even when the Union cracked
and furious blood
ran north and south
along the lines of pillage.
Secession grieved him
like the falling-out of brothers.
After Appomattox he laid
the white flower of forgiving
on Lee's crisp sword.
What was there left for him to do?
When the curtain rose
on *Our American Cousin*
he leaned forward in his chair
toward the last absurdity,
that other laughable country,
for which he was ready with his ransom —
a five-dollar Confederate note
in mint condition, and nine
newspaper accolades
neatly folded in his wallet.
It was time for him now
to try on his gold-rimmed spectacles,
the pair with the sliding temples
mended with a loop of string,
while the demon of the absolute,
who had been skulking in the wings,
leaped into focus,
waving a smoking pistol.

In the Great Hall of the Library,
as in a glass aquarium,
Abe Lincoln is swimming around,
dressed to the nines
in his stovepipe hat
and swallowtail coat,
effortlessly swimming,
propelled by sudden little kicks
of his gunboat shoes.
His billowing pockets hang
inside out; he is swimming
around, lighter at each turn,
giddy with loss,
while his memory sifts
to the sticky floor.
He is slipping away from us
into his legend and his fame,
having relinquished, piece by piece,
what he carried next to his skin,
what rocked to his angular stride,
partook of his man-smell,
shared the intimacy of his needs.
Mr. President,
in this Imperial City,
awash in gossip and power,
where marble eats marble
and your office has been defiled,
I saw the piranhas darting
between the rose-veined columns,
avid to strip the flesh
from the Republic's bones.
Has no one told you
how the slow blood leaks
from your secret wound?

4

To be old and to be young
again, inglorious private
in the kitchens of the war
that winter of blackout,
walking by the Potomac
in melancholy khaki,
searching for the prairie star,
westward scanning the horizon
for its eloquent and magnanimous light,
yearning to be touched by its fire:
to be touched again, with the years
swirling at my feet, faces
blowing in the wind
around me where I stand,
withered, in the Great Hall.

5

He steps out from the crowd
with his rawboned, warty look,
a gangling fellow in jeans
next to a plum-colored sari,
and just as suddenly he's gone.
But there's that other one
who's tall and lonely.

MEDITATIONS ON DEATH

—*from Giuseppe Ungaretti*

I

O sister of the shadow,
blackest in strongest light,
Death, you pursue me.

In a pure garden
innocent desire conceived you
and peace was lost,
pensive death,
on your mouth.

From that moment
I hear you in the mind's flow,
sounding the far depths,
suffering rival of eternity.

Poisonous mother of the ages,
fearful of palpitation
and of solitude,

beauty punished and smiling,
in the drowse of flesh
runaway dreamer,

unsleeping athlete
of our greatness,

when you have tamed me, tell me:
in the melancholy of the living
how long will my shadow fly?

II

Probing the deepest selves
of our unhappy mask
(enclosure of the infinite)
with fanatic blandishment —
the dark vigil of our fathers.

Death, mute word,
riverbed of sand deposited
by the blood,
I hear you singing like a locust
in the darkened rose of reflections.

III

Etcher of the secret wrinkles
in our unhappy mask —
the infinite jest of our fathers.

You, in the deep light,
O confused silence,
insist like the angry locusts.

IV

Clouds took me by the hand

On the hillside I burn space and time,
like one of your messengers,
like a dream, divine death.

V

You have closed your eyes.

A night is born
full of hidden wounds,

of dead sounds
as of corks
when the nets are let down to the water

Your hands become a breath
of inviolable distances,
slippery as thoughts,

And that equivocation of the moon
and that gentlest rocking,
if you would lay them on my eyes,
touch the soul.

You are the woman who passes by
like a leaf

leaving an autumn fire in the trees.

VI

O beautiful prey,
night-voice,
your movements
breed a fever.

Only you, demented memory,
could capture freedom.

On your elusive flesh
trembling in clouded mirrors
what crimes, I wonder,
did you not teach me to consummate?

With you, phantoms, I have no reticences,

and my heart is filled with your remorse
when it is day.

THE QUARREL

The word I spoke in anger
weighs less than a parsley seed,
but a road runs through it
that leads to my grave,
that bought-and-paid-for lot
on a salt-sprayed hill in Truro
where the scrub pines
overlook the bay.
Half-way I'm dead enough,
strayed from my own nature
and my fierce hold on life.
If I could cry, I'd cry,
but I'm too old to be
anybody's child.
Liebchen,
with whom should I quarrel
except in the hiss of love,
that harsh, irregular flame?

THE UNQUIET ONES

Years ago I lost
both my parents' addresses.
Father and mother lie
in their neglected cribs,
obscure as moles,
unvisited.
I do not need to summon them.
When I put out the light
I hear them stir, dissatisfied,
in their separate places,
in death as in life
remote from each other,
having no conversation
except in the common ground
of their son's mind.
They slip through narrow crevices
and, suddenly blown tall,
glide into my cave of phantoms,
unwelcome guests, but not
unloved, dark emissaries
of the two-faced god.

MY SISTERS

Who whispered, souls have shapes?
So has the wind, I say.
But I don't know,
I only feel things blow.

I had two sisters once
with long black hair
who walked apart from me
and wrote the history of tears.
Their story's faded with their names,
but the candlelight they carried,
like dancers in a dream,
still flickers on their gowns
as they bend over me
to comfort my night-fears.

Let nothing grieve you,
Sarah and Sophia.
Shush, shush, my dears,
now and forever.

ROUTE SIX

The city squats on my back.
I am heart-sore, stiff-necked,
exasperated. That's why
I slammed the door,
that's why I tell you now,
in every house of marriage
there's room for an interpreter.
Let's jump into the car, honey,
and head straight for the Cape,
where the cock on our housetop crows
that the weather's fair,
and my garden waits for me
to coax it into bloom.
As for those passions left
that flare past understanding,
like bundles of dead letters
out of our previous lives
that amaze us with their fevers,
we can stow them in the rear
along with ziggurats of luggage
and Celia, our transcendental cat,
past-mistress of all languages,
including Hottentot and silence.
We'll drive non-stop till dawn,
and if I grow sleepy at the wheel,

you'll keep me awake by singing
in your bravura Chicago style
Ruth Etting's smoky song,
"Love Me or Leave Me,"
belting out the choices.

Light glazes the eastern sky
over Buzzards Bay.
Celia gyrates upward
like a performing seal,
her glistening nostrils aquiver
to sniff the brine-spiked air.
The last stretch toward home!
Twenty summers roll by.

THE LAYERS

I have walked through many lives,
some of them my own,
and I am not who I was,
though some principle of being
abides, from which I struggle
not to stray.
When I look behind,
as I am compelled to look
before I can gather strength
to proceed on my journey,
I see the milestones dwindling
toward the horizon
and the slow fires trailing
from the abandoned camp-sites,
over which scavenger angels
wheel on heavy wings.
Oh, I have made myself a tribe
out of my true affections,
and my tribe is scattered!
How shall the heart be reconciled
to its feast of losses?
In a rising wind
the manic dust of my friends,
those who fell along the way,
bitterly stings my face.
Yet I turn, I turn,

exulting somewhat,
with my will intact to go
wherever I need to go,
and every stone on the road
precious to me.
In my darkest night,
when the moon was covered
and I roamed through wreckage,
a nimbus-clouded voice
directed me:
"Live in the layers,
not on the litter."
Though I lack the art
to decipher it,
no doubt the next chapter
in my book of transformations
is already written.
I am not done with my changes.

The Testing-Tree

———

1971

JOURNAL FOR MY DAUGHTER

1

Your turn. Grass of confusion.
You say you had a father once:
his name was absence.
He left, but did not let you go.
Part of him, more than a shadow,
beckoned down corridors,
secret, elusive, saturnine,
melting at your touch.
In the crack
of a divided house
grew the resentment-weed.
It has white inconspicuous flowers.
Family of anthologists!
Collectors of injuries!

2

I wake to a glittering world,
to the annunciation of the frost.
A popeyed chipmunk scurries past,
the pockets of his cheeks bulging.
As the field mice store seeds,
as the needle-nosed shrew
threading under the woodpile

deposits little heaps of land-snails
for milestones on its runways,
I propose
that we gather our affections.
Lambkin, I care.

3

I was happy you were born,
your banks of digits
equipped for decimals,
and all your clever parts
neatly in place.
Your nation gives me joy,
as it has always given.
If I could have my choice
on the way to exile
I think I'd rather sleep forever
than wake up cold
in a country without women.

4

You cried. You cried.
You wasted and you cried.
Night after night
I walked the floor with you,
croaking the same old
tranquillizing song,
the only tune
I ever learned to carry.
In the rosy tissue
of your brain,
where memory begins,
that theme is surely scored,

waiting till you need
to play it back.
There were three crows
sat on a tree
Sing Billy Magee Magaw.
You do not need to sing to me.
I like the sound of your voice
even when you phone from school
asking for money.

5

There was a big blond uncle-bear,
wounded, smoke-eyed, wild,
who shambled from the west
with his bags full of havoc.
He spoke the bears' grunt-language,
waving his paws
and rocking on his legs.
Both of us were drunk,
slapping each other on the back,
sweaty with genius.
He spouted his nonsense-rhymes,
roaring like a behemoth.
You crawled under the sofa.

6

Goodies are shaken
from the papa-tree:
Be what you are. Give
what is yours to give.
Have style. Dare.
Such a storm of fortune cookies!
Outside your room

stands the white-headed prowler
in his multiple disguises
who reminds you of your likeness.
Wherever you turn,
down whatever street,
in the fugues of appetite,
in the groin of nightmare,
he waits for you,
haggard with his thousand years.
His agents are everywhere,
his heart is at home
in your own generation;
the folded message in his hands
is stiff with dirt and wine-stains,
older than the Dead Sea Scrolls.
Daughter, read:
What do I want of my life?
More! More!

7

Demonstrations in the streets.
I am there not there,
ever uneasy in a crowd.
But you belong,
flaunting your home-made
insubordinate flag.
Why should I be surprised?
We come of a flinty maverick line.
In my father's time, I'm told,
our table was set in turn
for Maxim Gorky, Emma Goldman,
and the atheist Ingersoll.
If your slogan is mis-spelt
Don't tred on me!

still it strikes
parents and politicians down.
Noli me tangere! is what
I used to cry in Latin once.
Oh to be radical, young, desirable, cool!

8

Your first dog was a Pekinese,
fat and saucy Ko-San,
half mandarin, half mini-lion,
who chased milkmen and mailmen
and bit the tires of every passing car
till a U.S. Royal bit him back.
You sobbed for half an hour,
then romped to the burial service
in the lower garden
by the ferny creek.
I helped you pick the stones
to mark his shallow grave.
It was the summer I went away.
One night I carried you outdoors,
in a blitz of fireflies,
to watch your first eclipse.
Your far-off voice,
drugged with milk and sleep,
said it was a leaf
sliding over the light.

9

The night when Coleridge,
heavy-hearted,
bore his crying child outside,

he noted
that those brimming eyes
caught the reflection
of the starry sky,
and each suspended tear
made a sparkling moon.

THE ILLUMINATION

In that hotel my life
rolled in its socket
twisting my strings.
All my mistakes,
from my earliest
bedtimes,
rose against me:
the parent I denied,
the friends I failed,
the hearts I spoiled,
including at least
my own left ventricle —
a history of shame.
"Dante!" I cried
to the apparition
entering from the hall,
laureled and gaunt,
in a cone of light.
"Out of mercy you came
to be my Master
and my guide!"
To which he replied:
"I know neither the time
nor the way
nor the number on the door . . .
but this must be my room,

I was here before."
And he held up in his hand
the key,
which blinded me.

THREE FLOORS

Mother was a crack of light
and a gray eye peeping;
I made believe by breathing hard
that I was sleeping.

Sister's doughboy on last leave
had robbed me of her hand;
downstairs at intervals she played
Warum on the baby grand.

Under the roof a wardrobe trunk
whose lock a boy could pick
contained a red Masonic hat
and a walking stick.

Bolt upright in my bed that night
I saw my father flying;
the wind was walking on my neck,
the windowpanes were crying.

THE FLIGHT OF APOLLO

Earth was my home, but even there I was a stranger. This mineral crust. I walk like a swimmer. What titanic bombardments in those old astral wars! I know what I know: I shall never escape from strangeness or complete my journey. Think of me as nostalgic, afraid, exalted. I am your man on the moon, a speck of megalomania, restless for the leap toward island universes pulsing beyond where the constellations set. Infinite space overwhelms the human heart, but in the middle of nowhere life inexorably calls to life. Forward my mail to Mars. What news from the Great Spiral Nebula in Andromeda and the Magellanic Clouds?

2

I was a stranger on earth.
Stepping on the moon, I begin
the gay pilgrimage to new
Jerusalems
in foreign galaxies.
Heat. Cold. Craters of silence.
The Sea of Tranquillity
rolling on the shores of entropy.
And, beyond,
the intelligence of the stars.

AROUND PASTOR BONHOEFFER

THE PLOT AGAINST HITLER

Jittery, missing their cues,
Bach's glory jailed in their throats,
they were clustered round the piano
in the Biedermeier parlor,
sisters and brothers
and their brothers by marriage,
rehearsing a cantata
for Papa's seventy-fifth birthday.
Kyrie eleison: Night
like no other night, plotted
and palmed,
omega of terror,
packed like a bullet
in the triggered chamber.
Surely the men had arrived at their stations.
Through the staves of the music
he saw their target strutting,
baring its malignant heart.
Lord, let the phone ring!
Let the phone ring!

NEXT TO LAST THINGS

Slime, in the grains of the State,
like smut in the corn,

from the top infected.
Hatred made law,
wolves bred out of maggots
rolling in blood,
and the seal of the church ravished
to receive the crooked sign.
All the steeples were burning.
In the chapel of his ear
he had heard the midnight bells
jangling: *if you permit*
this evil, what is the good
of the good of your life?
And he forsook the last things,
the dear inviolable mysteries —
Plato's lamp, passed from the hand
of saint to saint —
that he might risk his soul in the streets,
where the things given
are only next to last;
in God's name cheating, pretending,
playing the double agent,
choosing to trade
the prayer for the deed,
and the deed most vile.
I am a liar and a traitor.

THE EXTERMINATION CAMP

Through the half-open door of the hut
the camp doctor saw him kneeling,
with his hands quietly folded.
"I was most deeply moved by the way
this lovable man prayed,
so devout and so certain
that God heard his prayer."

Round-faced, bespectacled, mild,
candid with costly grace,
he walked toward the gallows
and did not falter.
Oh but he knew the Hangman!
Only a few steps more
and he would enter the arcanum
where the Master
would take him by the shoulder,
as He does at each encounter,
and turn him round
to face his brothers in the world.

KING OF THE RIVER

If the water were clear enough,
if the water were still,
but the water is not clear,
the water is not still,
you would see yourself,
slipped out of your skin,
nosing upstream,
slapping, thrashing,
tumbling
over the rocks
till you paint them
with your belly's blood:
Finned Ego,
yard of muscle that coils,
uncoils.

If the knowledge were given you,
but it is not given,
for the membrane is clouded
with self-deceptions
and the iridescent image swims
through a mirror that flows,
you would surprise yourself
in that other flesh
heavy with milt,

bruised, battering towards the dam
that lips the orgiastic pool.

Come. Bathe in these waters.
Increase and die.

If the power were granted you
to break out of your cells,
but the imagination fails
and the doors of the senses close
on the child within,
you would dare to be changed,
as you are changing now,
into the shape you dread
beyond the merely human.
A dry fire eats you.
Fat drips from your bones.
The flutes of your gills discolor.
You have become a ship for parasites.
The great clock of your life
is slowing down,
and the small clocks run wild.
For this you were born.
You have cried to the wind
and heard the wind's reply:
"I did not choose the way,
the way chose me."
You have tasted the fire on your tongue
till it is swollen black
with a prophetic joy:
"Burn with me!
The only music is time,
the only dance is love."

If the heart were pure enough,
but it is not pure,

you would admit
that nothing compels you
any more, nothing
at all abides,
but nostalgia and desire,
the two-way ladder
between heaven and hell.
On the threshold
of the last mystery,
at the brute absolute hour,
you have looked into the eyes
of your creature self,
which are glazed with madness,
and you say
he is not broken but endures,
limber and firm
in the state of his shining,
forever inheriting his salt kingdom,
from which he is banished
forever.

THE MULCH

A man with a leaf in his head
watches an indefatigable gull
dropping a piss-clam on the rocks
to break it open.
Repeat. Repeat.
He is an inlander
who loves the margins of the sea,
and everywhere he goes he carries
a bag of earth on his back.
Why is he down in the tide marsh?
Why is he gathering salt hay
in bushel baskets crammed to his chin?
"It is a blue and northern air,"
he says, as if the shiftings of the sky
had taught him husbandry.
Birthdays for him are when he wakes
and falls into the news of weather.
"Try! Try!" clicks the beetle in his wrist,
his heart is an educated swamp,
and he is mindful of his garden,
which prepares to die.

ROBIN REDBREAST

It was the dingiest bird
you ever saw, all the color
washed from him, as if
he had been standing in the rain,
friendless and stiff and cold,
since Eden went wrong.
In the house marked For Sale,
where nobody made a sound,
in the room where I lived
with an empty page, I had heard
the squawking of the jays
under the wild persimmons
tormenting him.
So I scooped him up
after they knocked him down,
in league with that ounce of heart
pounding in my palm,
that dumb beak gaping.
Poor thing! Poor foolish life!
without sense enough to stop
running in desperate circles,
needing my lucky help
to toss him back into his element.
But when I held him high,
fear clutched my hand,

for through the hole in his head,
cut whistle-clean . . .
through the old dried wound
between his eyes
where the hunter's brand
had tunneled out his wits . . .
I caught the cold flash of the blue
unappeasable sky.

INDIAN SUMMER AT LAND'S END

The season stalls, unseasonably fair,
blue-fair, serene, a stack of golden discs,
each disc a day, and the addition slow.
I wish you were here with me to walk the flats,
towards dusk especially when the tide is out
and the bay turns opal, filled with rolling fire
that washes on the mouldering wreck offshore,
our mussel-vineyard, strung with bearded grapes.
Last night I reached for you and shaped you there
lying beside me as we drifted past
the farthest seamarks and the watchdog bells,
and round Long Point throbbing its frosty light,
until we streamed into the open sea.
What did I know of voyaging till now?
Meanwhile I tend my flock, small golden puffs
impertinent as wrens, with snipped-off tails,
who bounce down from the trees. High overhead,
on the trackless roads, skywriting V and yet
another V, the southbound Canada express
hoots of horizons and distances. . . .

SUMMER SOLSTICE

—from Osip Mandelstam

Orioles live in the elms, and in classical verse
the length of the vowels alone determines the measure.
Once and once only a year nature knows quantity
stretched to the limit, as in Homer's meter.

O this is a day that yawns like a caesura:
serene from the start, almost painfully slowed.
Oxen browse in the field, and a golden languor
keeps me from drawing a rich, whole note from my reed.

TRISTIA

— *from Osip Mandelstam*

I made myself an expert in farewells
by studying laments, the nightfall of a woman's hair.
Oxen chew their cud; anticipation lags;
it is the town's last restless hour;
and I praise that ritual night when the cocks crowed
and eyelids, heavy with the griefs that pass,
opened to the light, while her weeping flowed
into the sound of the Muses singing.

Who knows, when the time comes to say goodbye,
what separation we are meant to bear
and what for us cockcrow shall signify
when the acropolis burns like a flare,
and why, at the new daybreak of a life,
when the ox is ruminating in his stall,
the herald cock, prophetic of rebirth,
should flap his wings on the town wall?

I bless the craft of spinning: the to-and-fro
action of the shuttle, the way the spindle hums.
Look! barefooted Delia, light as a feather,
hurries to meet you, flying as she comes.
Oh, how scrawny is the language of joy,
that weak foundation of our mortal lot!

Everything happened before; it will happen again.
Only the flash of recognition brings delight.

Be it so: a small transparent puppet lies,
like a dried squirrel-skin
extended on a plate,
while a girl crouches, staring, over the image.
Wax is for women what bronze is for men.
We, who move blindly toward a world of shades,
only in battle dare confront our fate, —
but their gift is to die while telling fortunes.

AFTER THE LAST DYNASTY

Reading in Li Po
how "the peach blossom follows the water"
I keep thinking of you
because you were so much like
Chairman Mao,
naturally with the sex
transposed
and the figure slighter.
Loving you was a kind
of Chinese guerrilla war.
Thanks to your lightfoot genius
no Eighth Route Army
kept its lines more fluid,
traveled with less baggage,
so nibbled the advantage.
Even with your small bad heart
you made a dance of departures.
In the cold spring rains
when last you failed me
I had nothing left to spend
but a red crayon language
on the character of the enemy
to break appointments,
to fight us not
with his strength

but with his weakness,
to kill us
not with his health
but with his sickness.

Pet, spitfire, blue-eyed pony,
here is a new note
I want to pin on your door,
though I am ten years late
and you are nowhere:
Tell me,
are you still mistress of the valley,
what trophies drift downriver,
why did you keep me waiting?

RIVER ROAD

That year of the cloud, when my marriage failed,
I slept in a chair, by the flagstone hearth,
fighting my sleep,
and one night saw a Hessian soldier
stand at attention there in full
regalia, till his head broke into flames.
My only other callers were the FBI
sent to investigate me as a Russian spy
by patriotic neighbors on the river road;
and flying squirrels parachuting from the elms
who squeaked in rodent heat between the walls
and upstairs rumbled at their nutty games.
I never dared open the attic door.
Even my nervous Leghorns joined the act,
indulging their taste for chicken from behind.
A glazed look swam into the survivors' eyes;
they caught a sort of dancing-sickness,
a variation of the blind staggers,
that hunched their narrow backs, and struck
a stiffened wing akimbo,
as round and round the poultry yard
they flapped and dropped and flapped again.
The county agent shook his head:
not one of them was spared the cyanide.

That year of the cloud, when my marriage failed,
I paced up and down the bottom-fields,

tamping the mud-puddled nurslings in
with a sharp blow of the heel
timed to the chop-chop of the hoe:
red pine and white, larch, balsam fir,
one stride apart, two hundred to the row,
until I heard from Rossiter's woods
the downward spiral of a veery's song
unwinding on the eve of war.

Lord! Lord! who has lived so long?
Count it ten thousand trees ago,
five houses and ten thousand trees,
since the swallows exploded from Bowman Tower
over the place where the hermit sang,
while I held a fantail of squirming roots
that kissed the palm of my dirty hand,
as if in reply to a bird.
The stranger who hammers No Trespass signs
to the staghorn sumac along the road
must think he owns this property.
I park my car below the curve
and climbing over the tumbled stones
where the wild foxgrape perseveres,
I walk into the woods I made,
my dark and resinous, blistered land,
through the deep litter of the years.

THE MAGIC CURTAIN

I

At breakfast mother sipped her buttermilk,
    her mind already on her shop,
    unrolling gingham by the yard,
stitching her dresses for the Boston trade.
Behind her, Frieda with the yellow hair,
    capricious keeper of the toast,
    buckled her knees, as if she'd lost
balance and platter, then winked at me, blue-eyed.
Frieda, my first love! who sledded me to sleep
    through snows of the Bavarian woods
    into the bell-song of the girls,
with kinds of kisses mother would not dream;
tales of her wicked stepfather, a dwarf,
    from whom she fled to Bremerhaven
    with scarcely the tatters on her back;
riddles, nonsense, lieder, counting-songs. . . .
    Eins, zwei, drei, vier, fünf, sechs, sieben,
    Wo ist denn mein liebster Herr geblieben?
    Er ist nicht hier, er ist nicht da,
    Er ist fort nach Amerika.
"Be sure," said mother briskly at the door,
    "that you get Sonny off to school
    on time. And see that he combs his hair."
How could she guess what we two had in mind?

Downtown at the Front St. Bi-jo (spelt Bijou)
   we were, as always, the first in line,
   with a hot nickel clutched in hand,
impatient for *The Perils of Pauline,*
my Frieda in her dainty blouse and skirt,
   I in my starched white sailor suit
   and buttoned shoes, prepared to hang
from cliffs, twist on a rack, be tied to rails.
School faded out at every morning reel,
   The Iron Claw held me in thrall,
   Cabiria taught me the Punic Wars,
at bloody Antietam I fought on Griffith's side.
And Keystone Kops came tumbling on the scene
   in outsized uniforms, moustached,
   their thick-browed faces dipped in flour,
to crank tin lizzies that immediately collapsed.
John Bunny held his belly when he laughed,
   ladies politely removed their hats,
   Cyrus of Persia stormed the gates,
upsetting our orgy at Belshazzar's Feast.
Then Charlie shuffled in on bunioned feet.
   We twirled with him an imaginary cane
   and blew our noses for the gallant poor
who bet on a horse, the horse that always loses.
Blanche Sweet, said Frieda, had a pretty name,
   but I came back with Arline Pretty,
   and, even sweeter, Louise Lovely.
Send me your picture, Violet Mersereau!
Lights up! Ushers with atomizers ranged
   the aisles, emitting lilac spray.
   We lunched on peanuts and Hershey bars
and moved to the Majestic for the two o'clock show.

3

Five . . . four . . . three . . . two . . . one . . .
>The frames are whirling backward, see!
>The operator's lost control.
Your story flickers on your bedroom wall.
Deaths, marriages, betrayals, lies,
>close-ups of tears, forbidden games,
>spill in a montage on a screen,
with chases, pratfalls, custard pies, and sores.
You have become your past, which time replays,
>to your surprise, as comedy.
>That coathanger neatly whisked your coat
right off your back. Soon it will want your skin.
>*Five . . four . . three . . two . . one . .*
>*Where has my dearest gone?*
>*She is nowhere to be found,*
>*She dwells in the underground.*
Let the script revel in tricks and transformations.
>When the film is broken, let it be spliced
>where Frieda vanished one summer night
with somebody's husband, daddy to a brood.
And with her vanished, from the bureau drawer,
>the precious rose-enameled box
>that held those chestnut-colored curls
clipped from my sorrowing head when I was four.
After the war an unsigned picture-card
>from Dresden came, with one word: *Liebe*.
>"I'll never forgive her," mother said,
but as for me, I do and do and do.

THE SYSTEM

That pack of scoundrels
tumbling through the gate
emerges
as the Order of the State.

HAND-ROLLED CIGARETTES

— from Yevgeny Yevtushenko

If, in a fisherman's hut, you poke
behind the sagging sideboard with a stick,
you'll find his stock for making cigarettes,
a pile of newspapers, many-years-thick.

There you'll meet mobs of secret agents
and doctor-poisoners of the age.
Bedbugs and roaches with moustaches
huddle, and crawl along the page.

Returning late, the tired fisherman
enjoys his ladled kvass's tang,
and sifts tobacco at his ease
onto some bureaucrat's harangue.

Cool in the practice of his skill,
with fingers confident and strong,
he coils the speech in a narrow tube
and neatly wets it with his tongue.

The contents? — they're not his affair!
That glowing edge of nicotine
advancing, at the end of day,
eats up the newsprint, line by line.

He would have liked a sunny day,
wind in his sails and a lucky catch.
His yellow nail gleams salmon-bright,
flicking dead words reduced to ash.

Old eulogies and exposés
fulfill their destiny and rise,
with trashy articles and poems,
in spiral columns to the skies.

When evening falls in the north country,
cigarette-tips pinpoint the gray,
as, caught in the mood of dirty weather,
fishermen sit and puff away.

Their worn tobacco pouches rustle
till dawn sweeps inland on the tide.
Listen! they roll another cigarette:
and history is on their side.

THE CUSTOMS COLLECTOR'S REPORT

For the sake of the record:
      on Tuesday, the 19th instant,
the third day of the storm,
      shortly before nightfall,
they swam over the pass together,
      this pair in their battered armor,
first seen in my spyglass;
      stovepipes assisting each other,
cylinders skating the snowcrust,
      comedians sprawling,
now and then dropping
      under the surface,
perceptible only
      as mounds in the driftage.

To whom, in this trial,
      could I turn for instructions?

At the north wall of the gorge,
      where zero poured to its funnel,
in the absence of guidelines
      I dared the encounter,
half-digging them out
      from the coils of the blizzard,
half-dying of cold
      as I scratched at the ice pack.

Then came issue of smothered voices,
      wind rumbling in empty barrels,
the sound of flags flapping
      in a cave of the mountain;
and the words that I heard
      flew by in tatters:
"nothing . . . nothing to declare . . .
      our wounds speak . . . heroes . . .
unfairly ambushed . . . the odds impossible . . .
      let our countrymen know . . . pride . . .
        honor . . .
how bravely . . . and oh
      what a body-count! . . ."
And the thinner voice cried,
      plaintively winding,
"True, brother, true! but tell me —
      what was the name of our war?"
When I lifted their helmets
      a gas escaped from them,
putrid, as from all battlefields,
      the last breath of the human.
That moment they were lightened.
      It seemed the earth shuddered,
the white tombs opened,
      disgorging their breastplates.
I saw them rise in the wind
      and roll off like ashcans.

Dear sirs, my lords, this
      is a lonely post,
what can I ask but your compassion?
      I petition you for transfer.

THE GLADIATORS

They fought in heavy armor
or, nimbly, with net and trident;
if lucky, against wild beasts,
but mostly against their brothers.

Criminals, captives, slaves,
what did they have to lose?
And the cheers egged them on,
as they waded through shit and blood.

When Claudius gave the sign
the throats of the fallen were cut
in the shade of the royal box:
he fancied their dying looks.

Domitian's coarser itch
was to set cripples on cripples.
No entertainment matched
the sport of their hacking and bleating.

Trajan's phantasmagoric show,
lasting a hundred days,
used up five thousand pairs
of jocks — and the count resumes.

A monk climbs out of the stands,
he is running onto the field,
he is waving his scrawny arms
to interrupt the games.

The mob tears him to bits.
Tomorrow the gates will be closed,
but the promised Crusades will start
with a torchlight children's parade.

BOLSHEVIKS

— from Aba Stolzenberg

They came on ponies, barefoot,
brandishing guns that had no bullets;
wore ladies' hats backwards; their leaders
with the look of deacons; and packs
of ox-men, heads wrapped in sacks.

They came in early autumn, shook down
the pears they could not pick by hand;
sprawled across sidewalks and church steps
and felt themselves masters of the land.

The motorcycles spring out of nowhere.
A blast from the roaring White Guards!
Of Trotsky's soldiers nothing remains here
but some sad little mounds near the woods.

THE MOUND BUILDERS

"Macon is the seventh layer of civilization on this spot."
— inscription at Ocmulgee National Monument, Georgia

I

Let the old geezers jig on Penn-
sylvania Avenue, and when the jig ends
let them offer a cracked tune
in praise of power:
the State counts the teeth of its friends.
All month, knee-deep in South,
oiled by Methodist money,
I have whirled to a different music
with oversweet, underdeveloped girls
who make me missionary.
My daughter sits in every class;
love is the tongue in my mouth.
Today through the streets of the Greek Revival
and the confederacy of the lawns
trumpeting with azaleas,
my rented Falcon flies
from the tiresome sound of my own voice,
the courteous chicken sitting on my plate,
and Sidney Lanier's exhausted flute
stuck in its cabinet of glass.
What's best in me lives underground,
rooting and digging, itching for wings;
my very worst imaginings

77

I give to the spoilers of the air.
At the National Park under a sky
of unshattered, unshatterable blue
I rejoice in the prevalence of green
and the starry chickweed of the fields;
through the millennial ordeal
part, if only part of me, goes down
to the master farmers who built this mound,
this ceremonial earth-lodge,
and locked an eagle in it, shaped of clay,
the fork-eyed spotted bird of their cult,
and piled their dead in mounds higher and higher,
and raised up temple-mounds
to the giver of breath and corn
on which they stacked the harvest fire
that lit this stage for two hundred years.
Fifteen square miles! They must have known their power
stopped by the willows at the river's edge,
and yet it was too much to hold:
only their ghost-song haunts the field.

2

Musician of the lost tribes,
you summon to the council chamber,
to the elders in their scooped-out circle,
an earth-faced chorus of the lost,
people without name to remember,
led by stallion-proud Emperor Brim
bearing his feathered calumet,
chief of the tall Cowetas,
father of the Creek Nation,
by the Spaniards called "Gran Cazique,"
most feared redman of his generation;
foreshadowed, as a scroll unwinds,

by potters out of the swamps
who set their mark on the fanciful pipes they smoked
in the figure of birds or humans,
makers of bowls with carinated shoulders;
and their distant cousins, a patient cloud,
upholding jars with a smooth fold of the lip;
and, more dimly still, the shellfish eaters,
people of the stone axe,
who pitched their noisome camps
on their garbage heaps;
and straggling far behind,
out of primeval murk,
those wandering hunters in search of food
who crossed the land-bridge of the Bering Strait
and sliding over the glacier's edge
paved our first trails with their Mongol bones.
They followed the game that they pursued
into museums of prehistory,
featureless but for the fluted points
dropped from the bloodied mammoth's flanks.

3

The mounds rise up on every side
of a seven-layered world, as I stand
in the middle of the Ocmulgee fields,
by the Central of Georgia Railway track,
with the Creek braves under my feet
and the City of Macon at my back.

BORIS PASTERNAK

—from Anna Akhmatova

He who has compared himself to the eye of a horse
peers, looks, sees, identifies,
and instantly like molten diamonds
puddles shine, ice grieves and liquefies.

In lilac mists the backyards drowse,
and depots, logs, leaves, clouds above;
that hooting train, that crunch of watermelon rind,
that timid hand in a perfumed kid glove . . .

All's ringing, roaring, grinding, breakers' crash —
and silence all at once, release;
it means he is tiptoeing over pine needles,
so as not to startle the light sleep of space.

And it means he is counting the grains
in the blasted ears; it means
he has come again to the Daryal Gorge,
accursed and black, from another funeral.

And again Moscow, where the heart's fever burns;
far off the deadly sleighbell chimes;
someone is lost two steps from home
in waist-high snow. The worst of times . . .

For spying Laocoön in a puff of smoke,
for making a song out of graveyard thistles,
for filling the world with a new sound
of verse reverberating in new space,

he has been rewarded by a kind of eternal childhood,
with the generosity and brilliance of the stars;
the whole of the earth was his to inherit,
and his to share with every human spirit.

DANTE

. . . mio bel San Giovanni
—from Anna Akhmatova

Even after his death he did not return
to the city that nursed him.
Going away, this man did not look back.
To him I sing this song.
Torches, night, a last embrace,
outside in her streets the mob howling.
He sent her a curse from hell
and in heaven could not forget her.
But never, in a penitent's shirt,
did he walk barefoot with lighted candle
through his beloved Florence,
perfidious, base, and irremediably home.

CLEOPATRA

—from Anna Akhmatova

She had already kissed Antony's dead lips,
she had already wept on her knees before Caesar . . .
and her servants have betrayed her. Darkness falls.
The trumpets of the Roman eagle scream.

And in comes the last man to be ravished by her beauty —
such a tall gallant! — with a shamefaced whisper:
"You must walk before him, as a slave, in the triumph."
But the slope of her swan's neck is tranquil as ever.

Tomorrow they'll put her children in chains. Nothing
remains except to tease this fellow out of mind
and put the black snake, like a parting act of pity,
on her dark breast with indifferent hand.

THE ARTIST

His paintings grew darker every year.
They filled the walls, they filled the room;
eventually they filled his world —
all but the ravishment.
When voices faded, he would rush to hear
the scratched soul of Mozart
endlessly in gyre.
Back and forth, back and forth,
he paced the paint-smeared floor,
diminishing in size each time he turned,
trapped in his monumental void,
raving against his adversaries.
At last he took a knife in his hand
and slashed an exit for himself
between the frames of his tall scenery.
Through the holes of his tattered universe
the first innocence and the light
came pouring in.

THE BOTTOM OF THE GLASS

Not by planning and not by choosing
I learned the mastery.
What a damnable trade
where winning is like losing!
The wheel keeps spinning,
the thread gets broken,
my hand cannot tell
its work from its loafing.
Life aims at the tragic:
what makes it ridiculous?
In age as in youth
the joke is preposterous.
And nothing shall save me
from meanness and sinning
but more of the same,
more losing like winning.

THE PORTRAIT

My mother never forgave my father
for killing himself,
especially at such an awkward time
and in a public park,
that spring
when I was waiting to be born.
She locked his name
in her deepest cabinet
and would not let him out,
though I could hear him thumping.
When I came down from the attic
with the pastel portrait in my hand
of a long-lipped stranger
with a brave moustache
and deep brown level eyes,
she ripped it into shreds
without a single word
and slapped me hard.
In my sixty-fourth year
I can feel my cheek
still burning.

AN OLD CRACKED TUNE

My name is Solomon Levi,
the desert is my home,
my mother's breast was thorny,
and father I had none.

The sands whispered, *Be separate,*
the stones taught me, *Be hard.*
I dance, for the joy of surviving,
on the edge of the road.

AGAIN! AGAIN!

Love knocked again at my door:
I tossed her a bucket of bones.
From each bone springs a soldier
who shoots me as a stranger.

THE TESTING-TREE

I

On my way home from school
    up tribal Providence Hill
        past the Academy ballpark
where I could never hope to play
    I scuffed in the drainage ditch
        among the sodden seethe of leaves
hunting for perfect stones
    rolled out of glacial time
        into my pitcher's hand;
then sprinted lickety-
    split on my magic Keds
        from a crouching start,
scarcely touching the ground
    with my flying skin
        as I poured it on
for the prize of the mastery
    over that stretch of road,
        with no one no where to deny
when I flung myself down
    that on the given course
        I was the world's fastest human.

Around the bend
    that tried to loop me home
        dawdling came natural
across a nettled field
    riddled with rabbit-life
        where the bees sank sugar-wells
in the trunks of the maples
    and a stringy old lilac
        more than two stories tall
blazing with mildew
    remembered a door in the
        long teeth of the woods.
All of it happened slow:
    brushing the stickseed off,
        wading through jewelweed
strangled by angel's hair,
    spotting the print of the deer
        and the red fox's scats.

Once I owned the key
    to an umbrageous trail
        thickened with mosses
where flickering presences
    gave me right of passage
        as I followed in the steps
of straight-backed Massassoit
    soundlessly heel-and-toe
        practicing my Indian walk.

3

Past the abandoned quarry
    where the pale sun bobbed
        in the sump of the granite,

past copperhead ledge,
    where the ferns gave foothold,
        I walked, deliberate,
on to the clearing,
    with the stones in my pocket
        changing to oracles
and my coiled ear tuned
    to the slightest leaf-stir.
        I had kept my appointment.
There I stood in the shadow,
    at fifty measured paces,
        of the inexhaustible oak,
tyrant and target,
    Jehovah of acorns,
        watchtower of the thunders,
that locked King Philip's War
    in its annulated core
        under the cut of my name.
Father wherever you are
    I have only three throws
        bless my good right arm.
In the haze of afternoon,
    while the air flowed saffron,
        I played my game for keeps —
for love, for poetry,
    and for eternal life —
        after the trials of summer.

4

In the recurring dream
    my mother stands
        in her bridal gown

under the burning lilac,
    with Bernard Shaw and Bertie
        Russell kissing her hands;
the house behind her is in ruins;
    she is wearing an owl's face
        and makes barking noises.
Her minatory finger points.
    I pass through the cardboard doorway
        askew in the field
and peer down a well
    where an albino walrus huffs.
        He has the gentlest eyes.
If the dirt keeps sifting in,
    staining the water yellow,
        why should I be blamed?
Never try to explain.
    That single Model A
        sputtering up the grade
unfurled a highway behind
    where the tanks maneuver,
        revolving their turrets.
In a murderous time
    the heart breaks and breaks
        and lives by breaking.
It is necessary to go
    through dark and deeper dark
        and not to turn.
I am looking for the trail.
    Where is my testing-tree?
        Give me back my stones!

THE GAME

Let's spin the bottle
No I don't want to be kissed

Sometimes I feel my arm
Is turning into a tree

Or hardening to stone
Past memory of green

I've a long way to go
Who never learned to pray

O the night is coming on
And I am nobody's son

Father it's true
But only for a day

THIS GARLAND, DANGER

---

from

Selected Poems: 1928-1958

1958

THE SCIENCE OF THE NIGHT

I touch you in the night, whose gift was you,
My careless sprawler,
And I touch you cold, unstirring, star-bemused,
That have become the land of your self-strangeness.
What long seduction of the bone has led you
Down the imploring roads I cannot take
Into the arms of ghosts I never knew,
Leaving my manhood on a rumpled field
To guard you where you lie so deep
In absent-mindedness,
Caught in the calcium snows of sleep?

And even should I track you to your birth
Through all the cities of your mortal trial,
As in my jealous thought I try to do,
You would escape me — from the brink of earth
Take off to where the lawless auroras run,
You with your wild and metaphysic heart.
My touch is on you, who are light-years gone.
We are not souls but systems, and we move
In clouds of our unknowing
                              like great nebulae.
Our very motives swirl and have their start
With father lion and with mother crab.

Dreamer, my own lost rib,
Whose planetary dust is blowing
Past archipelagoes of myth and light,
What far Magellans are you mistress of
To whom you speed the pleasure of your art?
As through a glass that magnifies my loss
I see the lines of your spectrum shifting red,
The universe expanding, thinning out,
Our worlds flying, oh flying, fast apart.

From hooded powers and from abstract flight
I summon you, your person and your pride.
Fall to me now from outer space,
Still fastened desperately to my side;
Through gulfs of streaming air
Bring me the mornings of the milky ways
Down to my threshold in your drowsy eyes;
And by the virtue of your honeyed word
Restore the liquid language of the moon,
That in gold mines of secrecy you delve.
Awake!
          My whirling hands stay at the noon,
Each cell within my body holds a heart
And all my hearts in unison strike twelve.

GREEN WAYS

Let me not say it, let me not reveal
How like a god my heart begins to climb
The trellis of the crystal
In the rose-green moon;
Let me not say it, let me leave untold
This legend, while the nights snow emerald.

Let me not say it, let me not confess
How in the leaflight of my green-celled world
In self's pre-history
The blind moulds kiss;
Let me not say it, let me but endure
This ritual like feather and like star.

Let me proclaim it — human be my lot! —
How from my pit of green horse-bones
I turn, in a wilderness of sweat,
To the moon-breasted sibylline,
And lift this garland, Danger, from her throat
To blaze it in the foundries of the night.

WHEN THE LIGHT FALLS

When the light falls, it falls on her
In whose rose-gilded chamber
A music strained through mind
Turns everything to measure.

The light that seeks her out
Finds answering light within,
And the two join hands and dance
On either side of her skin.

The lily and the swan
Attend her whiter pride,
While the courtly laurel kneels
To kiss his mantling bride.

Under each cherry-bough
She spreads her silken cloths
At the rumor of a wind,
To gather up her deaths,

For the petals of her heart
Are shaken in a night,
Whose ceremonial art
Is dying into light.

AMONG THE GODS

Within the grated dungeon of the eye
The old gods, shaggy with gray lichen, sit
Like fragments of the antique masonry
Of heaven, a patient thunder in their stare.

Huge blocks of language, all my quarried love,
They justify, and not in random poems,
But shapes of things interior to Time,
Hewn out of chaos when the Pure was plain.

Sister, my bride, who were both cloud and bird
When Zeus came down in a shower of sexual gold,
Listen! we make a world! I hear the sound
Of Matter pouring through eternal forms.

AS FLOWERS ARE

As flowers have wars that the philosophic eye
Stoops to behold, broils of the golden age
When honey dropped from the trees, and the bees perform
Their educated dance, we find our skins
In which to parable the act of love,
Contending, as at first, that the world might move.

Perfection caught in amber of our days
Jewels the life; on the offended thread
We hang the instants of the soul's surprise
When it is ravished by the absolute god,
Who comes in any shape that he may choose
But the expected one: as flowers tell lies.

Your lazy tongue that makes me think of bells
And soft Mediterranean afternoons
(As flowers shoot stars) rings out its heaven-changes
Till souls and gods pick clover in your lines
And what I carry through the giant grass
Mocks the profession of the comic ants.

Summer is late, my heart: the dusty fiddler
Hunches under the stone; these pummelings
Of scent are more than masquerade; I have heard
A song repeat, repeat, till my breath had failed.
As flowers have flowers, at the season's height,
A single color oversweeps the field.

THE WALTZER IN THE HOUSE

A sweet, a delicate white mouse,
A little blossom of a beast,
Is waltzing in the house
Among the crackers and the yeast.

O the swaying of his legs!
O the bobbing of his head!
The lady, beautiful and kind,
The blue-eyed mistress, lately wed,
Has almost laughed away her wits
To see the pretty mouse that sits
On his tiny pink behind
And swaying, bobbing, begs.

She feeds him tarts and curds,
Seed packaged for the birds,
And figs, and nuts, and cheese;
Polite as Pompadour to please
The dainty waltzer of her house,
The sweet, the delicate, the innocent white mouse.

As in a dream, as in a trance,
She loves his rhythmic elegance,
She laughs to see his bobbing dance.

SOTTO VOCE

Say to me only
Huntress of nerves
You too are lonely
For the language that saves

Heart be not alien
Come to me strange
In the breast of a felon
Whose prison is songs

Share with me always
Though fraction be cross
The instant of gallows
The kiss of the axe

GRAMMAR LESSON

Waking was laughing then,
Orations without words;
Wishing was present tense
And that meant motion towards.

"There's grammar in my bones!"
I parsed it slow and lazy;
Endearments came in pairs,
Making my homage easy;

Each substantive drank light,
Required no definition,
Embraced its opposite,
As even poet, nation;

Looking and liking twined,
Red lions dressed their loins,
The pockets of my sight
Jingled with brand-new coins

Till brightness, original day,
Creator-kissed, appeared,
With the usual angel, stiff,
Waving his guttural sword —

But how could I remember
So early in the morning
(I lucky in my bed
And loved) Old Adverb's warning?

SHE WEPT, SHE RAILED

She wept, she railed, she spurned the meat
Men toss into a muslin cage
To make their spineless doxy bleat
For pleasure and for patronage,
As if she had no choice but eat
The lewd bait of a squalid age.

That moment when the lights go out
The years shape to the sprawling thing,
A marmoset with bloodied clout,
A pampered flank that learns to sing,
Without the grace, she cried, to doubt
The postures of the underling.

I thought of Judith in her tent,
Of Helen by the crackling wall,
Of Cressida, her bone-lust spent,
Of Catherine on the holy wheel:
I heard their woman-dust lament
The golden wound that does not heal.

What a wild air her small joints beat!
I only poured the raging wine
Until our bodies filled with light,
Mine with hers and hers with mine,
And we went out into the night
Where all the constellations shine.

FOREIGN AFFAIRS

We are two countries girded for the war,
Whisking our scouts across the pricked frontier
To ravage in each other's fields, cut lines
Along the lacework of strategic nerves,
Loot stores; while here and there,
In ambushes that trace a valley's curves,
Stark witness to the dangerous charge we bear,
A house ignites, a train's derailed, a bridge
Blows up sky-high, and water floods the mines.
Who first attacked? Who turned the other cheek?
Aggression perpetrated is as soon
Denied, and insult rubbed into the injury
By cunning agents trained in these affairs,
With whom it's touch-and-go, don't-tread-on-me,
I-dare-you-to, keep-off, and kiss-my-hand.
Tempers could sharpen knives, and do; we live
In states provocative
Where frowning headlines scare the coffee cream
And doomsday is the eighth day of the week.

Our exit through the slammed and final door
Is twenty times rehearsed, but when we face
The imminence of cataclysmic rupture,
A lesser pride goes down upon its knees.
Two countries separated by desire! —
Whose diplomats speed back and forth by plane,

Portmanteaus stuffed with fresh apologies
Outdated by events before they land.
Negotiations wear them out: they're driven mad
Between the protocols of tears and rapture.

Locked in our fated and contiguous selves,
These worlds that too much agitate each other,
Interdependencies from hip to head,
Twin principalities both slave and free,
We coexist, proclaiming Peace together,
Tell me no lies! We are divided nations
With malcontents by thousands in our streets,
These thousands torn by inbred revolutions.
A triumph is demanded, not moral victories
Deduced from small advances, small retreats.
Are the gods of our fathers not still daemonic?
On the steps of the Capitol
The outraged lion of our years roars panic,
And we suffer the guilty cowardice of the will,
Gathering its bankrupt slogans up for flight
Like gold from ruined treasuries.
And yet, and yet, although the murmur rises,
We are what we are, and only life surprises.

THE UNWITHERED GARLAND

Her grace is not of any part,
But selfhood's self, its very motion,
The mortal dream surprised by art
More effortless than wind or ocean,
All spirit flowing out to burn
The essence of its contradiction,
And give more light the more it turn.
Things are not only what they are:
They pass beyond themselves to learn
The tears of the particular.
If she go ranging out of sight
To suffer on a distant star
Her wounding by the infinite,
It is in answer to her law.
Who had of her the world's delight
And loved her for her sacred flaw
Loves her not less beyond his reach,
Still with the wonder that he saw
Alive. Perfectly to pray,
As the Fathers of the Desert teach,
He does not even try to pray.

THE MAN UPSTAIRS

The old man sick with boyhood fears,
Whose thin shanks ride the naked blast,
Intones; the gray somnambulist
Creaks down interminable stairs,
Dreaming my future as his past.

A flower withers in its vase,
A print detaches from the wall,
Beyond the last electric bill
Slow days are crumbling into days
Without the unction of farewell.

Tonight there suffers in my street
The passion of the silent clerk
Whose drowned face cries the windows dark
Where once the bone of mercy beat.
I turn; I perish into work.

O Magus with the leathern hand,
The wasted heart, the trailing star,
Time is your madness, which I share,
Blowing next winter into mind . . .
And love herself not there, not there.

THE APPROACH TO THEBES

In the zero of the night, in the lipping hour,
Skin-time, knocking-time, when the heart is pearled
And the moon squanders its uranian gold,
She taunted me, who was all music's tongue,
Philosophy's and wilderness's breed,
Of shifting shape, half jungle-cat, half-dancer,
Night's woman-petaled, lion-scented rose,
To whom I gave, out of a hero's need,
The dolor of my thrust, my riddling answer,
Whose force no lesser mortal knows. Dangerous?
Yes, as nervous oracles foretold
Who could not guess the secret taste of her:
Impossible wine! I came into the world
To fill a fate; am punished by my youth
No more. What if dog-faced logic howls
Was it art or magic multiplied my joy?
Nature has reasons beyond true or false.
We played like metaphysic animals
Whose freedom made our knowledge bold
Before the tragic curtain of the day:
I can bear the dishonor now of growing old.

Blinded and old, exiled, diseased, and scorned —
The verdict's bitten on the brazen gates,
For the gods grant each of us his lot, his term.
Hail to the King of Thebes! — my self, ordained

To satisfy the impulse of the worm,
Bemummied in those famous incestuous sheets,
The bloodiest flags of nations of the curse,
To be hung from the balcony outside the room
Where I encounter my most flagrant source.
Children, grandchildren, my long posterity,
To whom I bequeath the spiders of my dust,
Believe me, whatever sordid tales you hear,
Told by physicians or mendacious scribes,
Of beardless folly, consanguineous lust,
Fomenting pestilence, rebellion, war,
I come prepared, unwanting what I see,
But tied to life. On the royal road to Thebes
I had my luck, I met a lovely monster,
And the story's this: I made the monster me.

THE DARK AND THE FAIR

A roaring company that festive night;
The beast of dialectic dragged his chains,
Prowling from chair to chair in the smoking light,
While the snow hissed against the windowpanes.

Our politics, our science, and our faith
Were whiskey on the tongue; I, being rent
By the fierce divisions of our time, cried death
And death again, and my own dying meant.

Out of her secret life, that griffin-land
Where ivory empires build their stage, she came,
Putting in mine her small impulsive hand,
Five-fingered gift, and the palm not tame.

The moment clanged: beauty and terror danced
To the wild vibration of a sister-bell,
Whose unremitting stroke discountenanced
The marvel that the mirrors blazed to tell.

A darker image took this fairer form
Who once, in the purgatory of my pride,
When innocence betrayed me in a room
Of mocking elders, swept handsome to my side,

Until we rose together, arm in arm,
And fled together back into the world.

What brought her now, in the semblance of the warm,
Out of cold spaces, damned by colder blood?

That furied woman did me grievous wrong,
But does it matter much, given our years?
We learn, as the thread plays out, that we belong
Less to what flatters us than to what scars;

So, freshly turning, as the turn condones,
For her I killed the propitiatory bird,
Kissing her down. Peace to her bitter bones,
Who taught me the serpent's word, but yet the word.

THE THIEF

In a Roman tram, where the famous Roman mob,
Wrung from the bowels of the hippodrome,
Mauled into shape its many-elbowed god
To fight for exit through its civil wars,
Somebody Roman picked my pocket clean.
A pagan and a Christian curse on him!
Somebody Roman, may he find tonight
In the street of the serpents or the lion's mouth,
Strewn on a wine-soaked board,
More than he reached for, more than cash,
Green trumpeters, for whom the legions march
Through solid stone. (Meanwhile the Carthaginians
Play redskins in the ambush of the sea
To whom must be meted out the standard destruction:
It is a heavy responsibility.)
                        Let the *ladrone* sneer
As the leathered fold yields him my haunt of years,
The papers of a life I wanted lost,
Memos, addresses, the snapshot of a child,
To plague him through his alley nights until
He begs for mercy for the thing well-robbed.
Worlds in my pocket older than his own,
May they erupt on him like hissing gold,
Tooth of the pythoness, chimaera's scales,

Stones of the temple and Isaiah's beard —
Toss him, sweet furies, from Tarpeia's Rock!

More even than my purse,
And that's no laughing matter, it is my pride
That has been hurt: a fine Italian hand,
With its mimosa touch, has made me feel
Blind-skinned, indelicate, a fool Americano
Touring a culture like a grand museum,
People and statues interchangeable shows,
Perception blunted as one's syntax fails.

Why am I here? Some thirty years ago
A set of lantern slides I saw at school
Of these antiquities gave me an image
Of the rare serene that brimmed my eyes,
For nothing pleased me then in my legacy;
But the past that tempted me, the frozen pure,
Was a pedagogic lie. All's motion here,
And motion like emotion is impure,
A flower flawed by mutability,
Religion by its ruins, and yet thereby
More lovely and more graced, perhaps
More true. Still, still, the chariot wheels
Turn, the assassin motorcyclists charge,
Wolves prowl in the streets under arcades of bells,
Tiberius grovels through his dungeon halls
Dreaming of boy-sized fishes in his bath;
Behind the balcony of the Cardinal's palace,
Smelling the laureled Mamertine blood,
A baldpate awaits his rhetorical cue,
And the clouds drift
Through a triumph of broken columns.

Pick-pocket, pick-thank music plucks the strings

For the rag-madonna with perdurable babe
Most dolorously hallowing the square
Where Caesar walks three steps to meet Bernini,
Whose sumptuous art runs wild
From gate to gate, pausing in tiptoe-joy
Only to light a torch of fountains, to set
His tritons dancing, or at a blest façade
To cast up from his wrist a flight of angels,
Volute on volute, wing on climbing wing.
In the middle of my life I heard the waters playing.

Mater Cloaca, feast thee well, I pray,
On what has been subtracted from my fate —
Ten days of lectures, thirty days abroad:
In this excess that's Rome I'll not mope long,
Wearing my heart less Roman than baroque,
Though damn it all! I wish I'd lived in style,
Jogged in *carrozze* round and round the town,
Guzzled Spumante by the bucketful,
Bought wagons of daffodils to please my dear.
Now that I face the moment and the loss,
Driven to language on the Ides of March
Here in my blistered room
Where the wind flaps my ceiling like a sail
(A miracle, no doubt, to be left at that!)
I recognize the gods' capricious hand
And write this poem for money, rage, and love.

END OF SUMMER

An agitation of the air,
A perturbation of the light
Admonished me the unloved year
Would turn on its hinge that night.

I stood in the disenchanted field
Amid the stubble and the stones,
Amazed, while a small worm lisped to me
The song of my marrow-bones.

Blue poured into summer blue,
A hawk broke from his cloudless tower,
The roof of the silo blazed, and I knew
That part of my life was over.

Already the iron door of the north
Clangs open: birds, leaves, snows
Order their populations forth,
And a cruel wind blows.

GOOSE POND

Goose Pond's imaginable snows,
The fall of twenty years at once,
Like subtler moons reflect the rose
Decompositions of the sun.

A feather tumbling from a cloud
Scrolls thunders of the natural law;
The cattails rattle; cinnamon fern
Raises rag banners towards the thaw,

And early-footed ghost flowers scour
Through willow-dapplings to a cave
Where secrecy grows fur. Self burns
At the pulpits where Jack-preachers rave!

Now a sulky weather dogs the heart,
There is no bottom to the day,
The water lily's Chinese stalk
Drags heavy, as the white-lipped boy

Climbs from detritus of his birth,
The rusted hoop, the broken wheels,
The sunken boat of little worth,
Past balconies of limber eels

Until, along that marshy brink,
The springy trails devoid of plan,
He meets his childhood beating back
To find what furies made him man.

THE DRAGONFLY

Fallen, so freshly fallen
From his estates of air,
He made on the gritty path
A five-inch funeral car,
New Hampshire's lesser dragon
In the grip of his kidnapers.
A triumph of *chinoiserie*
He seemed, in green and gold
Enameling, pin-brained,
With swizzle-stick for tail,
The breastplate gemmed between.
What a gallantry of pomp
In that royal spread of wings! —
Four leaves of thinnest mica,
Or, better, of the skin
Of water, if water had a skin.
Semaphores, at rest,
Of the frozen invisible,
They caught a glinting light
In the hairlines of their scripture
When a vagrom current stirred
And made them feign to flutter.
It was a slow progress,
A thing of fits and starts,
With bands of black attendants
Tugging at the wings

And under the crested feelers
At the loose-hinged head
(So many eyes he had, which were
The eyes?), still others pushing
From behind, where a pair
Of ornamental silks
That steered him in his flights
Gave tenuous pincer-hold.
Admire, I said to myself,
How he lords it over them,
Grounded though he may be
After his blue-sky transports;
But see how they honor him,
His servants at the feast,
In a passion of obsequies,
With chomping mandibles
And wildly waving forelegs
Telegraphing news abroad
Of their booty's worth; oh praise this
Consummate purity
Of the bestriding will!
In a scaled-down mythology
These myrmidons could stand
For the separate atoms of St. George
(Why not?). And fancy drove
Me on, my science kneeling
Before such witless tools,
To pay my tithe of awe
And read the resurrection-sign
In the motion of the death.
But then I saw,
When an imperceptible gust
Abruptly hoisted sails
And flipped my hero over . . .
In the reversal of the scene

I saw the sixfold spasm
Of his tucked-in claws,
The cry of writhing nerve-ends,
And down his membrane-length
A tide of gray pulsation.
I wheeled. The scorpion sun,
Stoking its belly-fires,
Exploded overhead, and the rain
Came down: scales, tortuous wires,
Flakings of green and gold.

THE WAR AGAINST THE TREES

The man who sold his lawn to standard oil
Joked with his neighbors come to watch the show
While the bulldozers, drunk with gasoline,
Tested the virtue of the soil
Under the branchy sky
By overthrowing first the privet-row.

Forsythia-forays and hydrangea-raids
Were but preliminaries to a war
Against the great-grandfathers of the town,
So freshly lopped and maimed.
They struck and struck again,
And with each elm a century went down.

All day the hireling engines charged the trees,
Subverting them by hacking underground
In grub-dominions, where dark summer's mole
Rampages through his halls,
Till a northern seizure shook
Those crowns, forcing the giants to their knees.

I saw the ghosts of children at their games
Racing beyond their childhood in the shade,
And while the green world turned its death-foxed page

And a red wagon wheeled,
I watched them disappear
Into the suburbs of their grievous age.

Ripped from the craters much too big for hearts
The club-roots bared their amputated coils,
Raw gorgons matted blind, whose pocks and scars
Cried Moon! on a corner lot
One witness-moment, caught
In the rear-view mirrors of the passing cars.

THE THING THAT EATS THE HEART

The thing that eats the heart comes wild with years.
It died last night, or was it wounds before,
But somehow crawls around, inflamed with need,
Jingling its medals at the fang-scratched door.

We were not unprepared: with lamp and book
We sought the wisdom of another age
Until we heard the action of the bolt.
A little wind investigates the page.

No use pretending to the pitch of sleep;
By turnings we are known, our times and dates
Examined in the courts of either/or
While armless griefs mount lewd and headless doubts.

It pounces in the dark, all pity-ripe,
An enemy as soft as tears or cancer,
In whose embrace we fall, as to a sickness
Whose toxins in our cells cry sin and danger.

Hero of crossroads, how shall we defend
This creature-lump whose charity is art
When its own self turns Christian-cannibal?
The thing that eats the heart is mostly heart.

BY LAMPLIGHT

Welcome, eccentric life,
Attracted to my star,
Let there be festival
Perverse and singular.
Let any drop of poison
Grow legs and crawl and eat:
The malice of unreason
A man can tolerate.
The stumblers and the clowns
Are wired with their will
To live, to live, to live:
They do not mean to kill.
Sweet beetles, comrade moths,
The bonfires in your head
Are neither coals of hell
Nor the rose in the marriage-bed.
I heard all summer long
(Dance, monsters, hairy forms!)
The idiot on the leaf
Babbling of dust and storms,
And in this rough heart made
A little thin-legged song
Out of my greening blood
To swell the night's harangue.

THE SCOURGE

My heart felt need to die,
Our dusty time had come;
I said, "Endure the lie,
The waste, the tedium."

My heart sank to his knees,
Schooled in the tragic style,
But I, being out of heart,
Whipped him another mile,

And not because I cared
To let that actor go,
But only that I feared
His eternal No, No, No.

Beyond the covered bridge
The crooked road turned wild;
He rose at the season's edge,
Passionate and defiled,

Plucking the remnant leaf
Stained with the only good,
While all my children leaped
Out of the glowing wood.

OFF POINT LOTUS

Three years I lolled in that country of the girls,
Thick with their wine, their loose idolatry,
Nor saw that I was only prince of gulls,
Nor heard the ambiguous whisper of the sea.

Used . . . used! Eating their morphine leaf,
I breathed a cloud of self-congratulations
To pillow me, while my boat slapped on the wharf
And a gang of spiders scribbled invitations.

All right, my bully-boys, you who connived
My fall, I thank you for your dirty part,
I kiss you for each lie you took to wife
And for that salt you packed around my heart.

Good-bye, old things, I do not mourn you lost.
My crazy vessel dances to the rail,
Sea-drunken since I left that barbarous coast,
The stain of anger spreading on my sail.

ROVER

How shall I keep this violence in,
My no-name and my nothing-knows,
Original with fire and sin,
My mastiff breed? Citizens, close
Your doors; be warned; a man has lost
His dog, suspected to be mad,
Last seen prevailing down the coast
From Boston Light to Trinidad;
Biter of joys, a beast apart,
Sucked on the cold teat of the will,
Rolled in the ordure of the heart,
Gorged on the discontents that kill.

"Rover!" I call my fourfoot home,
Whose only language is a growl;
Dig up old bones, but he won't come
That chose the world: it is more foul.

HERMETIC POEM

The secret my heart keeps
Flows into cracked cups.

No saucer can contain
This overplus of mine:

It glisters to the floor,
Lashing like lizard fire

And ramps upon the walls
Crazy with ruby ills.

Who enters by my door
Is drowned, burned, stung, and starred.

TO THE READER

—from Charles Baudelaire: "Au Lecteur"

Ignorance, error, cupidity, and sin
Possess our souls and exercise our flesh;
Habitually we cultivate remorse
As beggars entertain and nurse their lice.

Our sins are stubborn. Cowards when contrite
We overstuff confession with our pains,
And when we're back again in human mire
Vile tears, we think, will wash away our stains.

Thrice-potent Satan in our cursèd bed
Lulls us to sleep, our spirit overkissed,
Until the precious metal of our will
Is vaporized — that cunning alchemist!

Who but the Devil pulls our waking-strings?
Abominations lure us to their side;
Each day we take another step to hell,
Descending through the stench, unhorrified.

Like an exhausted rake who mouths and chews
The martyrized breast of an old withered whore

We steal, in passing, whatever joys we can,
Squeezing the driest orange all the more.

Packed in our brains incestuous as worms
Our demons celebrate in drunken gangs,
And when we breathe, that hollow rasp is Death
Sliding invisibly down into our lungs.

If the dull canvas of our wretched life
Is unembellished with such pretty ware
As knives or poison, pyromania, rape,
It is because our soul's too weak to dare!

But in this den of jackals, monkeys, curs,
Scorpions, buzzards, snakes — this paradise
Of filthy beasts that screech, howl, grovel, grunt —
In this menagerie of mankind's vice

There's one supremely hideous and impure!
Soft-spoken, not the type to cause a scene,
He'd willingly make rubble of the earth
And swallow up creation in a yawn.

I mean *Ennui!* who in his hookah-dreams
Produces hangmen and real tears together.
How well you know this fastidious monster, reader,
— Hypocrite reader, you — my double! my brother!

THE WAY DOWN

I

Time swings her burning hands
I saw him going down
Into those mythic lands
Bearing his selfhood's gold,
A last heroic speck
Of matter in his mind
That ecstasy could not crack
Nor metaphysics grind.
I saw him going down
Veridical with bane
Where pastes of phosphor shine
To a cabin underground
Where his hermit father lives
Escaping pound by pound
From his breast-buckled gyves;
In his hermit father's coat,
The coat without a seam,
That the race, in its usury, bought
For the agonist to redeem,
By dying in it, one
Degree a day till the whole
Circle's run.

2

When the magician died, I wept,
I also died, I under leaf forgot
The stars, the distaff, and the crystal bowl.
I hugged the ignorance of stone
Under the line of the crickets' thunder
Where the white chariot of the winter sun
Raced to the axle pole.
Why am I suddenly warm all over?
By the small mouths of the rain
I'm tempted. Must I learn again to breathe?
Help me, my worldlings, leave
To the hoot owl in the dismal wood
His kingdom of blight
And empty branching halls.
Air thickens to dirt.
Great hairy seeds that soar aloft
Like comets trailing tender spume
Break in the night with soft
Explosions into bloom.
Where the fleshed root stirs,
Marvelous horned strong game,
Brine-scaled, dun-caked with mould,
Dynastic thunder-bison, Asian-crude,
Bedded in moss and slime,
Wake, and the rhythm of their blood
Shoots through the long veins of my name.
Hail, thickets! Hail, dark stream!

3

Time swings her burning hands.
The blossom is the fruit,
And where I walk, the leaves

Lie level with the root.
My brave god went from me.
I saw him going down
Incorrigibly wild
In a cloud of golden air.
O father in the wood,
Mad father of us all,
King of our antlered wills,
Our candelabrum-pride
That the pretender kills,
Receive your dazzling child
Drunk with the morning-dew
Into your fibrous love
Wherewith creation's strung
Although the last heart die;
Embrace him in our stead,
Keeping the old time young,
And hold him through the night
Our best hopes share, as bright,
As peerless as a cock's eye.

THE CLASS WILL COME TO ORDER

O tell me all about Anna Livia! I want to hear all about
Anna Livia.
Well, you know Anna Livia? Yes, of course, we all know
Anna Livia.
Tell me all. Tell me now. You'll die when you hear.
— Finnegans Wake
. . . ed io sorridendo li guardava, e nulla dicea loro.
— Vita Nuova

Amid that Platonic statuary, of athletes
Playing their passionate and sexless games,
The governors-to-be struck careless on the lawns,
The soldiers' monument, the sparrow-bronzes,
Through that museum of Corinthian elms
I walked among them in the
Soliloquy of summer, a gravel-scholar.

Our Irish friend had counseled silence first:
He did not mean the silence of the cowed,
But hold your tongue, sir, rather than betray.
Decorum is a face the brave can wear
In their desire to be invisible and so
To hear a music not prescribed, a tendril-tune
That climbs the porches of the ear,
Green, cool, like cucumber-vine.
What if the face starts threatening the man?
Then exile, cunning. Yes, old father, yes,
The newspapers were right,
Youth is general all over America,

The snow will not be falling till next winter,
There is no hurry yet to take my journey.
"The almonds bloom," she wrote. But will they hold,
While I remain to teach the alphabet
I still must learn, the alphabet on fire,
Those wizard stones? As always, where the text ends
Lurks the self, so shamed and magical. Away!
Who stays here long enough will stay too long.
Time snaps her fan, and there's her creature caught,
Fixed in the pleatings, fated to return,
As thin as paper in the mother-folds.
Absurd though it may seem,
Perhaps there's too much order in this world;
The poets love to haul disorder in,
Braiding their wrists with her long mistress hair,
And when the house is tossed about our ears,
The governors must set it right again.
How wise was he who banned them from his state!

O tell me a tale before the lecture-bell!
I swear, Artificer, I swear I saw
Their souls awaiting me, with notebooks primed.
The lesson for today, the lesson's what?
I must have known, but did not care to know.
There is a single theme, the heart declares,
That circumnavigates curriculum.
The letter in my pocket kissed my hand.
I smiled but I did not tell them,
I did not tell them why it was I smiled.

THE SUMMING-UP

When young I scribbled, boasting, on my wall,
No Love, No Property, No Wages.
In youth's good time I somehow bought them all,
And cheap, you'd think, for maybe a hundred pages.

Now in my prime, disburdened of my gear,
My trophies ransomed, broken, lost,
I carve again on the lintel of the year
My sign: *Mobility* — and damn the cost!

A CHOICE OF WEAPONS

Reviewing me without undue elation
A critic who has earned his reputation
By being always Johnny-on-the-spot
Where each contemporary starts to rot
Conceded me integrity and style
And stamina to walk a measured mile,
But wondered why a gang of personal devils
Need clank their jigging bones as public evils:

"The times are suited for the gay empiric,
The witty ironist, the casual lyric;
Apparently it's gristle-fare, not fat,
At certain tables: must we weep at that?
Though poets seem to rail at bourgeois ills
It is their lack of audience that kills.
Their metaphysics but reflects a folly:
'Read me or I'll be damned and melancholy.'
This poet suffers: that's his right, of course,
But we don't have to watch him beat his horse."

Sir, if appreciation be my lack,
You may appreciate me, front and back —
I won't deny that vaguely vulgar need:
But do not pity those whose motives bleed

Even while strolling in a formal garden.
Observe that tears are bullets when they harden;
The triggered poem's no water-pistol toy,
But shoots its cause, and is a source of joy.

REVOLVING MEDITATION

How much I disapprove of it!
How little I love it!
Though, contrariwise,
Can there be
Anything half as dear?
God knows I've had my joys,
Tasted the honey on the branch
And picked a sprig or two
Of accidental laurel
Along the way;
But why do I wake at the sound,
In the middle of the night,
Of the tread of the Masked Man
Heavy on the stairs,
And from the street below
The lamentation of the wounded glove?
Agh! I am sometimes weary
Of this everlasting search
For the drama in a nutshell,
The opera of the tragic sense,
Which I would gladly be rid of.
A shameless keyhole god
Keeps spying on my worst,
Incontinently glued
To the obscene dumb show
Of the debasers of currency

In the private cabinet,
The dealers of soiled cards
At their desperate game . . .
And the double-dealers,
The ambiguous ones with their smeared
Faces, the acrobatic dancers —
Those who stood
Naked with me,
Adorable, adored,
On the magnet-head
Of the same inexorable pin.
Why should I be bothered with it?
Imagination cries
That in the grand accountancy
What happens to us is false;
Imagination makes,
Out of what stuff it can,
An action fit
For a more heroic stage
Than body ever walked on.
I have learned,
Trying to live
With this perjured quid of mine,
That the truth is not in the stones,
But in the architecture;
Equally, I am not deceived
By the triumph of the stuffing
Over the chair.
If I must build a church,
Though I do not really want one,
Let it be in the wilderness
Out of nothing but nail-holes.
I listen, I am always listening,
In fear that something might get by,
To the grammar of the public places,

But I fly towards Possibility,
In the extravagantly gay
Surprise of a journey,
Careless that I am bound
To the flaming wheel of my bones,
Preferring to hear, as I
Am forced to hear,
The voice of the solitary
Who makes others less alone,
The dialogue of lovers,
And the conversation of two worms
In the beam of a house,
Their mouths filled with sawdust.

A SPARK OF LAUREL

This man, this poet, said,
"I've carried in my head
For twenty years and more
Some lines you wrote before
I knew the meaning of
Euripides or love" —
And gravely then intoned,
Lured from the underground
The greekness of my song
Still melancholy-young;
While she, long since forgotten,
For whom the song was written,
Burned wanton once again
Through centuries of rain,
Smiling, as she must do,
To keep her legend true,
And struck the mortal blow,
But not that blood could flow.
Ha! Once again I heard
The transubstantial word
That is not mine to speak
Unless I break, I break;
The spiral verb that weaves
Through the crystal of our lives,
Of myth and water made
And incoherent blood;

What sirens on the coast
Trilled to Ulysses lost,
And Agamemnon's thigh
Opened at length to cry:
This laurel-sparking rhyme
That we repeat in time
Until the fathers rest
On the inhuman breast
That is both fire and stone,
Mother and mistress, one.

from

Passport to the War

———

1944

REFLECTION BY A MAILBOX

When I stand in the center of that man's madness,
Deep in his trauma, as in the crater of a wound,
My ancestors step from my American bones.
There's mother in a woven shawl, and that,
No doubt, is father picking up his pack
For the return voyage through those dreadful years
Into the winter of the raging eye.

One generation past, two days by plane away,
My house is dispossessed, my friends dispersed,
My teeth and pride knocked in, my people game
For the hunters of man-skins in the warrens of Europe,
The impossible creatures of an hysteriac's dream
Advancing with hatchets sunk into their skulls
To rip the god out of the machine.

Are these the citizens of the new estate
To which the continental shelves aspire;
Or the powerful get of a dying age, corrupt
And passion-smeared, with fluid on their lips,
As if a soul had been given to petroleum?

How shall we uncreate that lawless energy?

Now I wait under the hemlock by the road
For the red-haired postman with the smiling hand

To bring me my passport to the war.
Familiarly his car shifts into gear
Around the curve; he coasts up to my drive; the day
Strikes noon; I think of Pavlov and his dogs
And the motto carved on the broad lintel of his brain:
"Sequence, consequence, and again consequence."

MY SURGEONS

My surgeons are a savage band,
Surely their patient is ill-fated.
Their tricks are coarse: the small sweet hand
I seized was wax, or amputated.
With the humiliated swollen-footed
And the lost persecuted their traps are baited.

Deftly they opened the brain of a child,
And it was full of flying dreams;
Father was prowling in a field
With speckled tongue and a collar of flame.
They labeled it "Polluted Streams,"
The body floating with the name.

They studied a prostrate fever-chart
With unmitigating eyes; one said,
"Bohemian germs, *Weltschmerz,* bad art
And Spanish fly. Off with his head."
Another, "Fascist. His boot is filled with blood."
They cut me up till I was red.

Lastly they squeezed out of my veins
The bright liquor of sympathy;
I lost the touch of souls, the reins
On white revenge, and I was free

Of pity, a solid man of snow.
But in the night to whom could I go?

Lie down with me, dear girl, before
My butcher-boys begin to rave.
"No hope for persons any more,"
They cry, "on either side of the grave."
Tell them I say the heart forgives
The world. Yes, I believe. In love.

THE TUTORED CHILD

Your mother, whom the mirror-world has claimed,
Plucks at the telltale hairs with violent hand
And thinks time backward to a brassy song,
Rolling the grape of hysteria under her tongue.

Your father, in whom two ambitions rave,
Like stations wrangling on the foreign wave
For spheres of influence, loathes the heart that blends
His guilty love; but the quarrel never ends.

You are of nature's bright unlucky brood,
Born of the drop of talent in your blood
Wherewith the gates of mystery are oiled.
Mortals will touch you and your taste be spoiled,

Witches in metals test you. I observe
Defeat, taking short cuts from nerve to nerve,
Climb through the narrow transom of your will;
And I weep, for having made you vulnerable.

My poor poor child whose terrors never cease,
Here is my pity penny. Buy you peace.

THE SIGNAL FROM THE HOUSE

I said to the watcher at the gate,
"They also kill who wait."

I cried to the mourner on the stair,
"Mother, I hate you for those tears."

To mistress of the ruined hall,
The keeper of the sacred heart,

I brought the mind's indifference
And the heavy marble of my face.

For these who were too much with me
Were secretly against me:

Hostages to the old life,
Expecting to be ransomed daily

And for the same fond reason
From the deep prison of their person,

Their lantern shining in the window
Had signaled me, like cry of conscience,

Insisting that I must be broken
Upon the wheel of the unforsaken.

FATHER AND SON

Now in the suburbs and the falling light
I followed him, and now down sandy road
Whiter than bone-dust, through the sweet
Curdle of fields, where the plums
Dropped with their load of ripeness, one by one.
Mile after mile I followed, with skimming feet,
After the secret master of my blood,
Him, steeped in the odor of ponds, whose indomitable love
Kept me in chains. Strode years; stretched into bird;
Raced through the sleeping country where I was young,
The silence unrolling before me as I came,
The night nailed like an orange to my brow.

How should I tell him my fable and the fears,
How bridge the chasm in a casual tone,
Saying, "The house, the stucco one you built,
We lost. Sister married and went from home,
And nothing comes back, it's strange, from where she goes.
I lived on a hill that had too many rooms:
Light we could make, but not enough of warmth,
And when the light failed, I climbed under the hill.
The papers are delivered every day;
I am alone and never shed a tear."

At the water's edge, where the smothering ferns lifted
Their arms, "Father!" I cried, "Return! You know

The way. I'll wipe the mudstains from your clothes;
No trace, I promise, will remain. Instruct
Your son, whirling between two wars,
In the Gemara of your gentleness,
For I would be a child to those who mourn
And brother to the foundlings of the field
And friend of innocence and all bright eyes.
O teach me how to work and keep me kind."

Among the turtles and the lilies he turned to me
The white ignorant hollow of his face.

WELCOME THE WRATH

Poor john, who joined in make of wrong
And guessed no guile, dare I complain? —
Or practice to endure the heart unstrung,
The waiting at the door too long,
Winter, wages, and self-disdain.

Endure? That is the dialect of love,
The greenhorn of the west, my late companion,
Now straggling crossfoot half-alive
Back to his country, with crazy sleeve
Flopping, like a shot pinion.

Let him endure. I'll not: not warp my vision
To square with odds; not scrape; not scamp my fiber,
Though pushed by spoilers of the nerves' precision,
Bothered by caterpillars of suspicion,
Hired by speculators in my gut and labor.

Wrath has come down from the hills to enlist
Me surely in his brindled generation,
The race of the tiger; come down at last
Has wrath to build a bonfire of these rags
With one wet match and all man's desolation.

NIGHT LETTER

The urgent letter that I try to write
Night after night to you to whom I turn,
The staunchless word, my language of the wound,
Begins to stain the page. Here in my room
With my unkenneled need, the Faustian dog
That chews my penitential bones, I hope
And do not hope, I pray and mock my prayer,
Twisting my coils, this dangling life of mine,
Now twelve years come of age, and me unpleased
With all my ways, my very littlest ones,
My part, my lines, unless you hold them dear.
Where is your ministry? I thought I heard
A piece of laughter break upon the stair
Like glass, but when I wheeled around I saw
Disorder, in a tall magician's hat,
Keeping his rabbit-madness crouched inside,
Sit at my desk and scramble all the news.
The strangest things are happening. Christ! the dead,
Pushing the membrane from their face, salute
The dead and scribble slogans on our walls;
Phantoms and phobias mobilize, thronging
The roads; and in the Bitch's streets the men
Are lying down, great crowds with fractured wills
Dumping the shapeless burden of their lives
Into the rivers where the motors flowed.

Of those that stood in my doorway, self-accused,
Besmeared with failure in the swamps of trade,

One put a gun in his examiner's hand,
Making the judgment loud; another squats
Upon the asylum floor and plays with toys,
Like the spiral of a soul balanced on a stone,
Or a new gadget for slicing off the thumb;
The rest whirl in the torment of our time.
What have we done to them that what they are
Shrinks from the touch of what they hoped to be?
"Pardon," I plead, clutching the fragile sleeve
Of my poor father's ghost returned to howl
His wrongs. I suffer the twentieth century,
The nerves of commerce wither in my arm;
Violence shakes my dreams; I am so cold,
Chilled by the persecuting wind abroad,
The oratory of the rodent's tooth,
The slaughter of the blue-eyed open towns,
And principle disgraced, and art denied.
My dear, is it too late for peace, too late
For men to gather at the wells to drink
The sweet water; too late for fellowship
And laughter at the forge; too late for us
To say, "Let us be good each to the other"?
The lamps go singly out; the valley sleeps;
I tend the last light shining on the farms
And keep for you the thought of love alive,
As scholars dungeoned in an ignorant age
Tended the embers of the Trojan fire.
Cities shall suffer siege and some shall fall,
But man's not taken. What the deep heart means,
Its message of the big, round, childish hand,
Its wonder, its simple lonely cry,
The bloodied envelope addressed to you,
Is history, that wide and mortal pang.

THE LAST PICNIC

The guests in their summer colors have fled
Through field and hedgerow. Come, let's pick
The bones and feathers of our fun
And kill the fire with a savage stick.

The figures of our country play,
The mocking dancers, in a swirl
Of laughter waved from the evening's edge,
Wrote finis to a pastoral.

Now the tongue of the military man,
Summoning the violent,
Calls the wild dogs out of their holes
And the deep Indian from his tent,

Not to be tamed, not to be stamped
Under. Earth-faced, behind this grove,
Our failures creep with soldier hearts,
Pointing their guns at what we love.

When they shall paint our sockets gray
And light us like a stinking fuse,
Remember that we once could say,
Yesterday we had a world to lose.

THE HEMORRHAGE

The people made a ring
Around the man in the park.
He was our banished king
Of blames and staunchless flows,
Exhibitor of the dark
Abominable rose;

Our chief, returned at last
From exile, with the grim
Stamina of the lost,
To show his sovereign hurt.
Wildly we dreaded him
And the strong god of his heart

Escaping, crawling down
Ditches where papers blow,
Smearing the sills of the town,
Strangling the hydra-drains
Coiled under. Stop! We know
How much a man contains.

We picnicked all that day,
Dishonored signs that nayed us,
Pulled marigolds, were gay
Before the apes, smashed glass.

Rifles could not have made us
Keep off the bloody grass;

For we were sick of crimes
Against us, and the head
Pitched on the absorbing Times,
And no one to accuse,
And nothing paid for, and we read,
We read that day what blotted out the news.

THE HARSH JUDGMENT

Inside, a hundred doors by which to leave;
Outside, you never can come in again.
The gesture made is woven in the sleeve,
The spiral echo sinks into the grain.
What died in me will warn me if you turn
Not to be tender-minded, though I burn,
In time so cruel, so difficult for love.

The burden of the personal, the life
By profit plowed, the tapping of our power —
You know the long rebellion and the spleen.
Last night, last year, with the tumbling of a leaf
The autumn came. Dark leaf from darker tower
Falls miles, deeper than coals, and still goes down.
Courage! That pity made our hearts unclean.

CONFIDENTIAL INSTRUCTIONS

When, on your dangerous mission gone,
You underrate our foes as dunces,
Be wary, not of sudden gun,
But of your partner at the dances;

Lest you be tamed in dead-end alleys
Where the mind's virtue drops from sight,
Loath to unlink from darling follies
Cuddled in houses of deceit;

Or cozened dearly by the bitch
Of souls, the international spy
Whirling in young men's arms, to each
Mistress, but in old carrion's pay.

THE ECONOMIST'S SONG

Come sit beneath the tariff walls
Among the scuttling unemployed,
The rodent pack; sing madrigals
Of Demos and the Cyprian maid
Bewildered by the golden grain,
While ships with peril in their hulls,
Deploying on the lines of trade,
Transport the future of gangrene.

THE OLD CLOTHES MAN

Have you any old clothes to sell?
The years make a stain you can't conceal,
Your fabric's eaten, you discard
That part of your life for which you cared.

You pluck a thread from your cuff: it winces
Straight to your shoulder. Ambition grieves
In trunks and bags; moth-featured, minces
From closets, beating empty sleeves.

History stagnates in your house.
I smelt the ruinous time, will buy
Your waste of talent. There's an ooze
Of souls too virulent to die

Contagious on the baffling walls.
You sit and watch the ceiling crack;
Horror sifts through and softly falls
From worlds beyond the zodiac.

You fear the unappeasable bone
That growls in your breast, and the mind's long feather,
The heart that imitates a stone
Until your hands grow fast together

And violence unstrings your voice.
I know what hangs behind your stair,
Spoiling with conscience and disuse:
The uniform you never wear,

The fitness and the pride, so vilely
Dishonored, the smiling target mouth,
Innocence ambushed, in the sharp volley
Reeling before the huntsmen of youth.

Therefore I come to mobilize
Your poor blind wounds, as in the coat,
The form betrayed, the defeated eyes,
My brother my groom, my dear recruit.

There will be skirmishing and loot
And fires to light our marches. Let
The enemies of life beware
When these old clothes go forth to war.

CARELESS LOVE

Who have been lonely once
Are comforted by their guns.
Affectionately they speak
To the dark beauty, whose cheek
Beside their own cheek glows.
They are calmed by such repose,
Such power held in hand;
Their young bones understand
The shudder in that frame.
Without nation, without name,
They give the load of love,
And it's returned, to prove
How much the husband heart
Can hold of it: for what
This nymphomaniac enjoys
Inexhaustibly is boys.

THE SUPPER BEFORE LAST

The intellectuals at the feast,
Emaciated on their fare,
Clap hands at the fabulous new beast
Upon the massive platter borne.
Their tongues rejoice, steeped in the rare
Juices of the unicorn;
While drunk with ptomaines now, the crow
That hoarsely to the table came,
Snatches at gobbets flung below,
And smirking in his greasy frock
Clamps beak on the honeyed mortal game
Under the dreaming hip and hock.

THE DAUGHTERS OF THE HORSELEECH

The daughters of the horseleech crying "Give! Give!"
Implore the young men for the blood of martyrs.
How shall we keep the old senator alive
Unless we satisfy his thirst for cultures?

Entreat the rat, the weasel, and the fox
To forage for a toothless master;
Have mercy, boys, on the monkey in his box;
Dear Judas goat, lead out the sheep to slaughter,

For if the warlock with the gilded claws
Withers away, and of his bones are waters,
Who will transmute our foreheads into brass
And who will keep his two charming daughters?

BETWEEN THE ACTS

Fate hired me once to play a villain's part.
I did it badly, wasting valued blood;
Now when the call is given to the good,
It is that knave who answers in my heart.

THIS DAY THIS WORLD

My architects, forsaking me,
Submit designs for a bombproof mansion;
My scholars of the fourth dimension
Complain they starve to death in three;
My correspondents write all day
The business of the enemy.

Tapped of their useful energies,
My soldiers pace the mind's frontier;
Engine recoils from engineer
And strikes at the courage in his eyes.
When shall my swarthy workmen rise,
Demand the power and the keys?

THE ILLUSIONIST

My name is sand: I make
Dumbshows on windowshades;
Wring hands; dissolve; swirl back;
Play furious, grim charades.
In airless room confined,
Thick with the curds of night,
I live upon my mind,
Am six-foot parasite;
Am envy, like a vein
Run dry; am hypocrite,
Whose bonecase (melted down)
Shimmers with scaly wit.
What have I not permitted?
What flagrant postures taken?
Nor shown the head matted
Nor the white forehead broken,
But parodied my life,
Assumed eccentric forms,
Retreated into leaf,
Made branches of my arms;
Groveled; ah, clung in hiding
To my father's rotten wall.

Kneel, spirit. At this beheading
Thy spongy faces fall.

INVOCATION

Soul of my soul, in the ancestral wood
Where all the trees were loosened of their leaves
I strayed, uncovering my winter form;

Webbed in a dream, stagnating like a worm,
Offensive to myself, to the gray bird-drifts
Melting from the boughs with rhyming calls;

Ancient and hoarse, beslimed, glued to a rock
Five hundred years, fainting, struggling with mist
Self-woven, issue of death, ghost of my name —

Heard then the pods clack hollow blistered skins
Where shaggy nest, where musty honeycomb
Tipped in the blowing summer of your fame,

And sleazy men in cabins underground
Rose up and sang. Gleam of their eyes! by day
Harsh solar gold, and night's bleached lunar stone.

Too long I knew attrition in the rains,
Endured the conjugations of the stars,
Yet, Circler, one incendiary vein

I have defended, purified, to slake
You in the burning, whose daemonic beak
The clasp of bone about my heart O break!

NO WORD

Through portal and through peristyle
Her phantom glides, whose secret mouth,
The absence of whose flagrant smile,
Hangs on my chimney like a wreath of cloud.

I prod the coals; my tortured faith
Kneels in the blaze on melting paws;
Jeweled with tears, the lonely beast
Bequeaths me irony and claws.

No message. May the mothering dark,
Whose benediction calms the sea,
Abater of the atrocious spark
Of love and love's anxiety,

Be kind; and may my self condone,
As surely as my judge reprieves,
This heart strung on the telephone,
Folded in death, whom no voice revives.

THE LAST QUESTION

Oh the good times! the laughter on the hill!
The parties down at Larry's in the spring!
Your sovereign pleasure, careless itself to save,
Goes naked at the heart. Touching, you bring
Rumors of heaven and its generous spoils
Here, even, where our hooded shadows rise
To play the stab-scene, the end of love,
While grief intones, ever the third that stays.
Now that your pity shines in other hall,
Now that your grain again comes to the mill,
Shall I be happy soon, shall I rejoice,
Or wrestle with that stranger whom you praise?

HOW LONG IS THE NIGHT?

On the anvil of love my flesh has been hammered out.
Indifferent, in the indifferent air,
I circulate and suck the star-space in.
No one is dear to me now,
Leastly myself that sickened in the night.
I would abandon this loose bag of bones
And walk between the world's great wounds, unpitying.

THE GUILTY MAN

The years of my life were odd that now are even.
Think! to be young, amused, and not a fool;
Playing the world's game — think! — with world's own rules,
And nothing lost, I think, I think . . . but years.
Heart against mouth is singing out of tune,
Night's whisperings and blanks betrayed; this is
The end of lies: my bones are angry with me.

Father, the darkness of the self goes out
And spreads contagion on the flowing air.
I walk obscurely in a cloud of dark:
Yea, when I kneeled, the dark kneeled down with me.
Touch me: my folds and my defenses fall;
I stand within myself, myself my shield.

Teach me my reasons, I would know their names,
Cry scandal, drive my secrets out, because
I hate the excellence that spoils the world.
So quit me now, you honorable men
Whose treason is to turn the conscience kind,
And do not turn until you hear a child.

THE FITTING OF THE MASK

"Again I come to buy the image fated."
"Your valued image, sir, and that's a pity,
Is gone, I mean the youth, the undefeated,
Whose falcon-heart, winged with the golden shout
Of morning, sweeps windward from his native city,
Crying his father's grief, his mother's doubt."

"You knew I cared, and that I'd come for him;
The traffic hindered me; you should have known."
"Ah there, that's bad! But my poor memory's dim
As a bell that rings the tide in; I lose track
Of things to keep and things to sell, and one
Can never be quite certain who'll come back."

"Enough! There was another face, a bright
Pathetic one I'll take, from whose wild stain
Of sympathy a man could borrow light."
"Our catalogue describes him 'Fool of Love,
Fragile and dear, tinctured with mortal pain,
Buys grain of his grain and eats the chaff thereof.'"

"Your cataloguer has the cynic touch,
But I'll forgive him. Is our business over?"
"Be patient, sir. You would not thank me much
Or recommend my baffling merchandise

If I should offer this unblessed believer,
This torn-cheek, with the chasm in his eyes."

"Old man, I'm in a hurry to proceed,
And everyone, you know, must wear a mask.
Give me a countenance to meet my need
Or malice will expose me at the dance."
"Oh sir, we'll try, but it's no easy task
To make adjustments to your circumstance;

And now, while my assistant turns the key
And in the windows now the lights go out,
For it is closing time irrevocably
Until new features sit upon the forms,
I'll sing a little ditty to the ghost
That occupies this world of empty frames.

[*Sings:*]
Good-fellow's lost among our Psychic Cases,
The Angry Man has turned a ghastly blue,
Munich exhausted all our Judas-faces,
And what are we to do, and what to do?
The Optimist was mangled in a sock,
The rats conferred and ate The Wandering Jew,
There's nothing left that's decent in our stock,
And what are we to do, and what to do?

But look! — here's something rare, macabre, a true
Invention of the time's insomniac wits.
Perhaps we ought to sell it to the zoo.
Go to the darkening glass that traps your shames
And tell me what you see."
                              "O Prince of Counterfeits,
This is the Self I hunted and knifed in dreams!"

THE RECKONING

"What have you done?"

Pigeon, who are to me
Language and light
And the long flight home,
Your question comes with coils
Like years behind,
Which I am crawling from.
Be patient with my wound:
Too long I lay
In the folds of my preparation,
Sinuous in the sun,
A golden skin,
All pride, sores, excretion,
Blazing with death. O child,
From my angry side
Tumbles this agate heart,
Your prize, veined with the root
Of guilty life,
From which flow love and art.

OPEN THE GATES

Within the city of the burning cloud,
Dragging my life behind me in a sack,
Naked I prowl, scourged by the black
Temptation of the blood grown proud.

Here at the monumental door,
Carved with the curious legend of my youth,
I brandish the great bone of my death,
Beat once therewith and beat no more.

The hinges groan: a rush of forms
Shivers my name, wrenched out of me.
I stand on the terrible threshold, and I see
The end and the beginning in each other's arms.

from

Intellectual Things

"For the tear is an intellectual thing."
— William Blake

———

1930

CHANGE

Dissolving in the chemic vat
Of time, man (gristle and fat),
Corrupting on a rock in space
That crumbles, lifts his impermanent face
To watch the stars, his brain locked tight
Against the tall revolving night.
Yet is he neither here nor there
Because the mind moves everywhere;
And he is neither now nor then
Because tomorrow comes again
Foreshadowed, and the ragged wing
Of yesterday's remembering
Cuts sharply the immediate moon;
Nor is he always: late and soon
Becoming, never being, till
Becoming is a being still.

Here, Now, and Always, man would be
Inviolate eternally:
This is his spirit's trinity.

GEOMETRY OF MOODS

Concentrical, the universe and I
Rotated on God's crystal axletree,

So perfectly adjusted in suspense
I could not mark our split circumference,

But sphere in sphere, devotion in devotion,
Was a thing of folding air, a windy motion.

My spinal pole, tipped with a globe of light,
Stretched long as time into the infinite,

And when I turned to look upon the face
Of love's incarnate form, tremendous space

Inclined upon her mouth, the natural nest
Where, throbbing like a bird, singed thought might rest.

Concentrical, the universe and I
Rotated on God's crystal axletree,

I core of the world, a bead in a ball of glass
So pure that only Nothing could be less.

Oh the earth ensphered me, liberal and warm,
When the curve of heaven was her sleeping arm.

Now cubical upon a fractured pole
It creaks, scraping the circle of my soul.

FOR THE WORD IS FLESH

O ruined father dead, long sweetly rotten
Under the dial, the time-dissolving urn,
Beware a second perishing, forgotten,
Heap fallen leaves of memory to burn
On the slippery rock, the black eroding heart,
Before the wedged frost splits it clean apart.

The nude hand drops no sacramental flower
Of blood among the tough upthrusting weeds.
Senior, in this commemorative hour,
What shall the quick commemorate, what deeds
Ephemeral, what dazzling words that flare
Like rockets from the mouth to burst in air?

Of hypochondriacs that gnawed their seasons
In search of proofs, Lessius found twenty-two
Fine arguments, Tolet gave sixty reasons
Why souls survive. And what are they to you?
And, father, what to me, who cannot blur
The mirrored brain with fantasies of Er,

Remembering such factual spikes as pierce
The supplicating palms, and by the sea
Remembering the eyes, I hear the fierce
Wild cry of Jesus on the holy tree,

Yet have of you no syllable to keep,
Only the deep rock crumbling in the deep.

Observe the wisdom of the Florentine
Who, feeling death upon him, scribbled fast
To make revision of a deathbed scene,
Gloating that he was accurate at last.
Let sons learn from their lipless fathers how
Man enters hell without a golden bough.

TWILIGHT

I wait. I deepen in the room.
Fed lions, glowing, congregate
In corners, sleep and fade. For whom
It may concern I, tawny, wait.

Time flowing through the window; day
Spilling on the board its bright
Last blood. Folding (big, gauzy, gray),
A moth sits on the western light.

Sits on my heart that, darkened, drips
No honey from its punctured core,
Yet feeds my hands and feeds my lips.
The Moon, the Moon, is at the door!

SINGLE VISION

Before I am completely shriven
I shall reject my inch of heaven.

Cancel my eyes, and, standing, sink
Into my deepest self; there drink

Memory down. The banner of
My blood, unfurled, will not be love,

Only the pity and the pride
Of it, pinned to my open side.

When I have utterly refined
The composition of my mind,

Shaped language of my marrow till
Its forms are instant to my will,

Suffered the leaf of my heart to fall
Under the wind, and, stripping all

The tender blanket from my bone,
Rise like a skeleton in the sun,

I shall have risen to disown
The good mortality I won.

Directly risen with the stain
Of life upon my crested brain,

Which I shall shake against my ghost
To frighten him, when I am lost.

Gladly, as any poison, yield
My halved conscience, brightly peeled;

Infect him, since we live but once,
With the unused evil in my bones.

I'll shed the tear of souls, the true
Sweat, Blake's intellectual dew,

Before I am resigned to slip
A dusty finger on my lip.

PARTICULAR LULLABY

Declines at evening from your eyes,
Like summer slipping down a tree,
Your noon-high pride: but not your wise,
Your sensitive pleased beauty.

The ebb of spirit from the vase
Of woman is the hurt extreme
Of conscious breath. Bewilder your thighs,
Wrap your long thought in a dream.

By image of all hush, a mist
Of blossom on the feminine bough,
Annul the runner of your wrist,
The small clock going in your brow.

On present time's derisive hope
Then break, O ever of your smile:
Sunbreak of lips, from radiant sleep,
Dazzle the perpetually meanwhile.

PROMISE ME

Only, when I am sudden loss
Of consequence for mind and stair,
Picking my dogged way from us
To whom, recessive in some where
Of recollection, with the cross
Fallen, the breast in disrepair:

Only, when loosening clothes, you lean
Out of your window sleepily,
And with luxurious, lidded mien
Sniff at the bitter dark — dear she,
Think somewhat gently of, between
Love ended and beginning, me.

STRANGE CALENDAR

Considered by the logical brief clock
That keeps no reckoning of blood's unreason,
I cannot board your minute at the dock
Of this perpetual departure; I cannot wake
Beside your name, for having welcomed light in a later
    season.

Suppose my punctual hat should not arrive
Tonight at that known corner where the eyes
Expect: if you should stand engraved with love
Until through annuals of space I came to wive
Your precarious dear doom — suppose, My Early One,
    suppose —

Or even should your bashful feet have fled,
Yet one of me, arrived, shall pace the square;
And one of me shall watch your not mine bed,
Breathing upon your sleep; another shall have laid
Himself in the revolving rock and, ageless, wait you there.

POEM

O Heart: this is a dream I had, or not a dream.
Lovingly, lovingly, I wept, but my tears did not rhyme.

In the year of my mother's blood, when I was born,
She buried my innocent head in a field, because the earth

Was sleepy with the winter. And I spoke the corn,
And I cried the clover up, with the dewy mouth of my mirth.

In the honey of summer my brain conceived: a child, I flowered
Over the maiden-stalks, drinking sweet upper light,

For I was intimate with the sun, till he devoured
Me utterly, O Heart, his tenderest neophyte.

So I died. Small gluttonous birds picked on my limpid brow,
My pale drooped feet were manacled with rushing worms;

And when I was sufficiently dead (Torturer Thou!)
I was born again. Dissolving, memory reforms

The cyclic hour I pulled life's bony root, slow inch
By inch, from its loamy trap; shrilly, like a mandrake, screamed

To rip the cord, suck liberal air, after the pinch
Of planetary rock. Womanly, a shadow combed

Her dark tremendous hair beyond the violet border
Of my sleep. Strong passionate hands I had, but could not find

The red position of her heart, nor the subtle order
Of her lips and breasts, nor the breathing cities of her mind.

Lovingly, lovingly, I wept for her absent eyes,
Large pity of her thought; I broke the spine of my pride

Upon a stone, seeing she did not recognize
My tears, because our sorrows did not coincide.

Softly grieving, ironic at the gates of horn,
I took my baffled head and buried it under the corn.

O Heart: this is a dream I had, or not a dream.

DECIDUOUS BRANCH

Winter, that coils in the thickets now,
Will glide from the fields; the swinging rain
Be knotted with flowers; on every bough
A bird will meditate again.

Lord, in the night if I should die,
Who entertained your thrilling worm,
Corruption wastes more than the eye
Can pick from this imperfect form.

I lie awake, hearing the drip
Upon my sill; thinking, the sun
Has not been promised; we who strip
Summer to seed shall be undone.

Now, while the antler of the eaves
Liquefies, drop by drop, I brood
On a Christian thing: unless the leaves
Perish, the tree is not renewed.

If all our perishable stuff
Be nourished to its rot, we clean
Our trunk of death, and in our tough
And final growth are evergreen.

THE WORDS OF THE PREACHER

Taking infection from the vulgar air
And sick with the extravagant disease
Of life, my soul rejected the sweet snare
Of happiness; declined
That democratic bait, set in the world
By fortune's old and mediocre mind.

To love a changing shape with perfect faith
Is waste of faith; to follow dying things
With deathless hope is vain; to go from breath
To breath, so to be fed
And put to sleep, is cheat and shame — because
By piecemeal living a man is doomed, I said.

For time with clever fingers ties the knot
Of life that is extended like a rope,
And bundling up the spinning of our thought
(The ribbons and the lace
That might have made a garment for the wind),
Constricts our substance to a cipher's space.

Into the middle of my thought I crept
And on the bosom of the angel lay,
Lived all my life at once; and oh I wept
At what I could foresee;
Upon his death-soft burning plumage wept
To vie with God for His eternity.

MENS CREATRIX

Brain, be ice,
A frozen bowl of thought,
Pure radius of the marble eye
That is time's central spot:
In cold eternal calm
Chasten the trembling thigh.

Brain, brain:
Be fever's sepulcher,
Entomb the noise of frightened blood,
That I may strictly hear
The truthful pulse of beauty
Beyond this evil good.

Mental womb,
Intelligence of tight
Precision: He comes, the sudden Lord,
A rhythmic Spike of Light,
To cleave you with that spike:
Himself, His flowing Word.

Strike, O Poem, Strike!

AMBERGRIS

This body, tapped of every drop of breath,
In vast corruption of its swollen pride,
Is perfected to be the whale of death;
Yet, I believe, the hand that plumbs its side
Will gather dissolution's sweet increase,
Exquisite fern of death — in nature, ambergris.

Meanwhile, thinking of love, I have been dressed
For such destruction. Though it surely break,
Come pluck the deep wild kernel of my breast,
That wafer of devotion, and partake
Of its compacted sweetness, till it bring
The soul to rise upon the fleshly wing.

If gentle hearts are scorned, in scorn of it
I shall immerse it in such bitterness,
Bathe every pulse in such an acid wit,
That from my mammoth, cold, and featureless
Event of age, my enemies will flee,
Whereas my friends will stay and pillage me.

APPROACH OF AUTUMN

The early violets we saw together,
Lifting their delicate swift heads
As if to dip them in the water, now wither,
Arching no more like thoroughbreds.

Slender and pale, they flee the rime
Of death: the ghosts of violets
Are running in a dream. Heart-flowering time
Decays, green goes, and the eye forgets.

Forgets? But what spring-blooded stock
Sprouts deathless violets in the skull
That, pawing on the hard and bitter rock
Of reason, make thinking beautiful?

THE PIVOT

He heard the centuries tick slowly,
Earth's pulse equivocate. *O Lord,*
Gigantic silence strikes: Thy holy
And undeniable Word.

This is the bitter promised day
When, dragging wings, he leaves behind
A faunlike head upon a tray,
Spear buried in the mind.

Now he must tread the starry wrack
And penetrate the burning sea.
Dearly beloved, I may come back,
But do not wait for me.

HE

He runs before the wise men: he
Is moving on the hills like snow.
No gifts, no tears, no company
He brings, but wind-rise and water-flow.

In meadows of descended day
His motion leans, dividing air:
He takes the unforgiving way
Beneath the apostolic star.

She who has known him calls him stranger.
Parting the night's long hair, he steals
Within the heart, that humble manger
Where the white, astonished spirit kneels.

His vertical inflicting pride,
Whose shadow cuts the nib of space,
Bends to this virtue fructified.
But though he kiss the little face

Like rapture breaking on the mind,
The necessary fierce details
Implacably he has designed.
Redemption hangs upon the nails.

VERY TREE

Forget the tube of bark,
Alliterative leaves,
Tenacious like a hand
Gnarled rootage in the dark
Interior of land.

Bright incidental bird
Whose melody is fanned
Among the bundled sheaves,
Wild spool of the winding word,
Reject: and let there be
Only tree.

Earth's absolute arithmetic
Of being is not in the flowering stick
Filled with the sperm of sun,
But in a figure seen
Behind our eyelids when we close
Slow petals of the brain
At evening like a rose.

Colors pour in and out:
Here is a timeless structure wrought
Like the candelabrum of pure thought,

Stripped of green root and leaf,
Getting no seed to sprout,

Yet lovely, lovely,
God's Very Tree,
Form of whose intense inner life
Abstractly branches to attain
What glory, Tree, what pain?

PROPHECY ON LETHE

Echo, the beating of the tide,
Infringes on the blond curved shore;
Archaic weeds from sleep's green side
Bind skull and pelvis till the four
Seasons of the blood are unified.

Anonymous sweet carrion,
Blind mammal floating on the stream
Of depthless sound, completely one
In the cinnamon-dark of no dream —
A pod of silence, bursting when the sun

Clings to the forehead, will surprise
The gasping turtle and the leech
With your strange brain blooming as it lies
Abandoned to the bipeds on the beach;
Your jelly-mouth and, crushed, your polyp eyes.

POSTSCRIPT

Darling, darling, by narrow ambages
Of fate, by gardens flowering with beasts,
I journeyed to this place. The forest marches
Behind the stalker, and the running grass
Steps lightly over his defeated bones.
This is the perilous way without return.
In glassy prison now of contemplation
I, fugitive from progress, leap erect
In analytic dance on time's acute
And bitter needle. Crueler than a spine
It penetrates the body till it pricks
The bubbling brain, exploding life's gray tumor
Together with its iridescent world.
I lost by winning, and I shall not win
Again except by loss. The smoky past,
Mixed with the wind, will not evaporate
Into the color of air. Let life be false,
But in our circular trap the blood remembers
Its throbbing on the lip; the hands observe
Communion, touching in the sleep of thought;
And the punctual heart reiterates love's name.
Some little comfort I have found to think
That, though this phoenix will not hatch an egg,
Yet will its lyric history be saved
In generations of its mental brood.
And I have found some little comfort too

In colloquy with death the quiet-eyed,
Our profound and inexhaustible old father,
Still loyal to his tall obedient sons.
I have been social with the pale abstractions
That congregate within a lethal room;
But these strict walls encounter me; this house
Exhales resentment of audacious hope.
A man can starve upon the golden-sweet
Impossible apples of Cézanne; a man
Can eagerly consult a woman's head
(Picasso's), but her slow and stupid eyes
Drink light in vegetative apathy.
O darling, a man can cry out to his love
All night and day, and still be comfortless.
The meaning of a mouth, a breast, is plain,
But what you mean to me is dipped in blood
And tangled like the bright threads of a dream.

LOVERS RELENTLESSLY

Lovers relentlessly contend to be
Superior in their identity:

The compass of the ego is designed
To circumscribe intact a lesser mind

With definition; tender thought would wrest
Each clean protective secret from the breast;

Affection's eyes go deep, make morbid lesion
In pride's tissue, are ferocious with possession;

Love's active hands are desperate to own
The subtly reasoned flesh on branching bone;

Lovers regard the simple moon that spills
White magic in a garden, bend their wills

Obliquely on each other; lovers eat
The small ecstatic heart to be complete;

Engaged in complicate analysis
Of passionate destruction, lovers kiss;

In furious involvement they would make
A double meaning single. Some must break

Upon the wheel of love, but not the strange,
The secret lords, whom only death can change.

DEATH IN MOONLIGHT

A leopard no more secret
Is than she who goes
By night alone, observing
Moon-foam upon the rose;

A doe is not more gentle
Than she who palely treads
Through peonies' white clusters,
Brushing small rabbit-heads;

Her steps are light as dewdrops
Among imagined sheep,
Timid that she may startle
A herd of rocks from sleep;

She tarries for a moment
Beside a sky-deep pond
To watch a floating turtle;
Enchanted, moves beyond

To greet a glittering forest,
A tall and starry town
That calls to her supple body,
"Come down! Come down!"

REGARD OF TANGENTS

The flesh has knowledge of the flesh.
Lean hip and deep familiar breast
Encounter opposites. Melodiously
Beats (O beats!) the bringing bird of wish.

So has the adult thirsty bread
Been dipped in song: still is a thirst
Intrinsic in the body's briefest crumb,
As shapes of thought go snuggling to a bed

Where double joy may singly lie,
Or once might probably have lain.
For love is coming or is passing by,
And none may look upon her features plain.

How shall these tarry, how shall these meet,
When he must remember and she forget?
Her baby-heart is running down a street
Already ended, his to a place not yet.

FOR PROSERPINE

Our purple tongues that testify
The pomegranate has been broken
Are stained, their roots and buds are stained, with the shy
Fruity pleasure of us, met, spoken.

(I shall remember the days
Of my youth and your beautiful new ways.)

In fierce decay I'll find a stripe
Of honey sweetening the tart
Old brain. I shall not know again such ripe
Beauty of the burst, dark heart.

(I'll think of my absurd,
Impossible, pledged, serious word.)

My undivulged interior world
A country for our souls shall be,
Till I am done with name and number, gnarled
And mindless like a babbling tree.

(A heavy bird will brood
On women stagnant in their blood.)

Preserve you from the long farewell
Whose sex is flowers, whose breasts are grain.

Return, return. Into a leafless hell
Gradually drops the brain.

(The bulls, the stallions, have tasted
Incredible fruit. Their seed is wasted.)

WHEN THE DEAD ARISE

When the dead arise,
(You know me, Lazarus)
When the resurrected generations climb
Into the orb of time,
Rubbing death from their eyes,

(O dark mad Lazarus)
When this maggoty dumb earth
Pronounces verbs erect and vertebrate,
Will the sexes flow with sweet
Wild honey of God's mirth?

Or will they stare
Bewildered at ascending noon;
Then turn, and leap with frightened hair
(Lazarus! Lazarus!)
In utter pits of marble sleep

Unbetrayably down.

PARTING

Parting, I take with me completed June,
My treasury of time, hoarded intact;
Eventual winds will not dissolve a tune
Of solid air, the body of this fact.
Mind's acres are forever green: Oh, I
Shall keep perpetual summer here; I shall
Refuse to let one startled swallow die,
Or, from the copper beeches, one leaf fall.

Here, wandered from confusion, I shall greet
My youth immaculate in memory's urn;
This is my country, where the tireless feet
Of my adventure, homing, will return.
Each day will end in this day; every ship
Will bring me back, bright lip on lonely lip.

I DREAMED THAT I WAS OLD

I dreamed that I was old: in stale declension
Fallen from my prime, when company
Was mine, cat-nimbleness, and green invention,
Before time took my leafy hours away.

My wisdom, ripe with body's ruin, found
Itself tart recompense for what was lost
In false exchange: since wisdom in the ground
Has no apocalypse or pentecost.

I wept for my youth, sweet passionate young thought,
And cozy women dead that by my side
Once lay: I wept with bitter longing, not
Remembering how in my youth I cried.

NIGHT-PIECE

And everywhere, all over, men have sighed
Good night, remembering of women the bright
Of eyes; put out their bodies like a light,
And set their brains adrift upon their blood.

Let us be shy again like feathered things,
Stroll in the gardens of the spectrum (all
Last summer). Waiting for the first snowfall,
Hear colors dropping, and the dark flurry of wings.

Prevent that deepmost dream. Think late, think soon,
Of crickets, Marvell, roses, and the bare
Shoulders of teasing Venus, and O the hair
Tumbling all over, everywhere, the moon.

Up ever so many stairs it is a new
Sweet (look! it's) morning in each other's arms.
Tell me, yes I truly, by what charms
Have I been, darling, yes I really do.

I think that it is so: but if I groan
Out of my middle sleep, believe I saw
The great fish tunneling the purple sea,
Earth-darkening bird that falls on man alone.

ME AND THE ROCK

Endlessly to no end wending
Pilgrim O my conscience in the green
Nacre of twilight abbreviate the heart

Autumn's beak is to the south
Death is north; westward one minute late
The plumed train leaps the shrilly stark ravine
Ever go feet go cars go the planes

Hearing the motors of the breast the brain
Loudly I wait their destinations wait

Coals of remembrance kissed and broken
These are the eyes; treasure the moment pure
Arrived at beauty impossible and vain

Now between me and the rock is
Now between me and myself is
Sight of the rock thought of myself: division sure

Then will the mouth of the air open
Cold slowly desolation pour over the blind
Punctures of sleep great gorges of the mind
Render me imperturbable to the rock
Deliver to myself completely me

TRANSFORMATIONS

All night he ran, his body air,
But that was in another year.

Lately the answered shape of his laughter,
The shape of his smallest word, is fire.

He who is a fierce young crier
Of poems will be tranquil as water,

Keeping, in sunset glow, the pure
Image of limitless desire;

Then enter earth and come to be,
Inch by inch, geography.

FIRST LOVE

At his incipient sun
The ice of twenty winters broke,
Crackling, in her eyes.

Her mirroring, still mind,
That held the world (made double) calm,
Went fluid, and it ran.

There was a stir of music,
Mixed with flowers, in her blood;
A swift impulsive balm

From obscure roots;
Gold bees of clinging light
Swarmed in her brow.

Her throat is full of songs,
She hums, she is sensible of wings
Growing on her heart.

She is a tree in spring
Trembling with the hope of leaves,
Of which the leaves are tongues.

LAST WORDS

Listen: from sleep's long pillow I arise
To go away. One moment let me lean
On falling air before I lock my eyes.
Are the leaves red now? No matter. Trees are green.

The colors of the world are permanent
Despite the bleach of change. Pure stain on stain,
The bow of light's eternal forms is bent
Across steep heaven in the general brain.

Who cries, The beautiful, the proud, are fallen!
(O silly child, it was myself that cried.)
Death, eater of the heads of flowers, spills pollen:
Our little strength, our beauty, and our pride

Are for the race to keep; we can discover
Secrets with our broken skulls; our dead feet run
Under the lid of earth that closes over
The generations marching to the sun.

EAGLE

The dwindling pole,
Tall perpendicular in air,
Attenuates to be a bird
Poised on a sphere.

No flag projects
This tensile grace, this needle-word,
Only, in rigid attitude,
The ball, the bird.

Metallic time
Has caught an eagle, trapped the beat
Of rushing wings, ensnared in bronze
His taloned feet.

Invader of
The thunder, never will you fly
Again to pluck the blazing heart.
Shall I? Shall I?

MOTION OF WISH

Through evolutions of the seed
To startled postures of the dead,
The motion of important wish
Is simpler than the motion of a fish
In water, or a bird in air.
Sprung from the brain, it will return there.
Possessed by objects, wish may find
Mastery only in the mind.
So when the sighing of the shoal,
The tropic birds, the monotonous roll
Of seasons over the island soul,
Confuse the bloodstream, mariners eat
One lotus-moment to forget
All other moments, and their eyes
Fasten on impossible surprise.
A man may journey to the sun,
But his one true love and companion
Sleeps curled in his thoughtful womb.
Here will the lone life-traveler come
To find himself infallibly home.

SO INTRICATELY IS THIS WORLD
RESOLVED

So intricately is this world resolved
Of substance arched on thrust of circumstance,
The earth's organic meaning so involved
That none may break the pattern of his dance;
Lest, deviating, he confound the line
Of reason with the destiny of race,
And, altering the perilous design,
Bring ruin like a rain on time and space.

Lover, it is good to lie in the sweet grass
With a dove-soft nimble girl. But O lover,
Lift no destroying hand; let fortune pass
Unchallenged, beauty sleep; dare not to cover
Her mouth with kisses by the garden wall,
Lest, cracking in bright air, a planet fall.

BENEDICTION

God banish from your house
The fly, the roach, the mouse

That riots in the walls
Until the plaster falls;

Admonish from your door
The hypocrite and liar;

No shy, soft, tigrish fear
Permit upon your stair,

Nor agents of your doubt.
God drive them whistling out.

Let nothing touched with evil,
Let nothing that can shrivel

Heart's tenderest frond, intrude
Upon your still, deep blood.

Against the drip of night
God keep all windows tight,

Protect your mirrors from
Surprise, delirium,

Admit no trailing wind
Into your shuttered mind

To plume the lake of sleep
With dreams. If you must weep

God give you tears, but leave
You secrecy to grieve,

And islands for your pride,
And love to nest in your side.

THE SEPARATION

Its narrow head that gnaws the breast
Is beautiful and bright,
Emblazoned with a jeweled crest,
Red plume of light.

The body of its reptile grace,
Glitter of gold and green,
Winds rippling in fastidious chase
Of heart's meat clean.

Who tears the serpent from the flesh
To stamp a bloody seal,
And laughs, inflicting gash on gash
With his iron heel,

Will thirst to fill in spirit's drought
The vacant well of pain,
And stoop to kiss the serpent's mouth,
And kiss in vain.

IN A STRANGE HOUSE

The memory of time is here imprisoned
In these walls, not fluent time that moves
Upon the flood, but time already reasoned
And undone of its quick eyes and loves.

We who are strangers in this finished house
Have slept with tossing shadows, and we lie
Astonished in our chambers lest we rouse
The strong assassins with a cry.

The dead would murder action. Oh, I know
Their subtle ways. They separate with fear
The fiery lips of thought. And I shall go
By silent lanes and leave you timeless here.

MASTER AND MISTRESS

As if I were composed of dust and air,
The shape confronting me upon the stair
(Athlete of shadow, lighted by a stain
On its disjunctive breast — I saw it plain —)
Moved through my middle flesh. I turned around,
Shaken, and it was marching without sound
Beyond the door; and when my hand was taken
From my mouth to beat the standing heart, I cried
My distant name, thinking myself had died.
One moment I was entered; one moment then
I knew a total century of pain
Between the twinkling of two thoughts. The ghost
Knocked on my ribs, demanding, "Host! Host!
I am diseased with motion. Give me bread
Before I quickly go. Shall I be fed?"
Yielding, I begged of him: "Partake of me.
Whatever runneth from the artery,
This body and its unfamiliar wine,
Stored in whatever dark of love, are thine."
But he denied me, saying, "Every part
Of thee is given, yea, thy flesh, thy heart."

ORGANIC BLOOM

The brain constructs its systems to enclose
The steady paradox of thought and sense;
Momentously its tissued meaning grows
To solve and integrate experience.
But life escapes closed reason. We explain
Our chaos into cosmos, cell by cell,
Only to learn of some insidious pain
Beyond the limits of our charted hell,
A guilt not mentioned in our prayers, a sin
Conceived against the self. So, vast and vaster
The plasmic circles of gray discipline
Spread outward to include each new disaster.
Enormous floats the brain's organic bloom
Till, bursting like a fruit, it scatters doom.

BEYOND REASON

The blessing in this conscious fruit, the hurt
Which is unanswerable, fill the brow
With early death. O Sion of my heart,
The milk of love were charitable now.

I do not come intent to be your lord,
Nor to contract the empire of your flight,
But as the long eye holds the spinning bird
Enclosed in the circumference of sight

And yet the bird is infinitely free
To dip its beak into the thinnest air,
So do I stand. I am not destiny
To color time or plot a hemisphere.

Creatures that carry in their little blood
Malignant influences moved to keep
Delight from love, the lonely from the proud,
Destroy themselves to live. If in my sleep

The ape, the serpent, and the fox I find
Shut with my soul in fortune's writhing sack,
I tame them with the sections of my mind
And teach my mind to love its thoughtless crack.

VITA NUOVA

I abdicate my daily self that bled,
As others breathe, for porridge it might sup.
Henceforth apocalypse will get my bread
For me. I bit my tongue and gnawed my lip,
But now the visor of my name is up.

Giving to love my undivided nature,
Kindling my fire, the spirit that I keep,
I have been otherwise a part-time creature,
With many selves to fool myself with hope,
And in myself a gentler self to weep.

Now I will peel that vision from my brain
Of numbers wrangling in a common place,
And I will go, unburdened, on the quiet lane
Of my eternal kind, till shadowless
With inner light I wear my father's face.

Moon of the soul, accompany me now,
Shine on the colosseums of my sense,
Be in the tabernacles of my brow.
My dark will make, reflecting from your stones,
The single beam of all my life intense.

NOTES
INDEX
―

NOTES

Page 2. *What of the Night?* Several of the details in Part 2 derive from Franz Kafka's story "The Country Doctor."

Page 4. *Quinnapoxet.* Quinnapoxet (also sometimes spelled with one *n*) was a backwater village outside Worcester, Massachusetts, where I spent my childhood summers as a boarder on the Buteau farm. The village no longer exists, and its place-name is all but forgotten.

Page 6. *Silence.* Bella Akhmadulina, born 1937, belongs to a great tradition of Russian woman poets, following in the footsteps of Anna Akhmatova and Marina Tsvetayeva. In the spring of 1977 she paid an unheralded visit to the United States. For her appearance at Queens College, New York, I translated and read this characteristic lyric of hers, together with other poems. We had previously read together at the University of Moscow in the spring of 1967.

Pages 8–14. *Words for the Unknown Makers.* Rose Slivka, editor of the periodical *Craft Horizons,* gave me *carte blanche* to write on the unprecedented exhibition "The Flowering of American Folk Art 1776–1876," at the Whitney Museum of American Art, New York, February 1 to March 24, 1974. This suite of poems, with photographic illustrations from the exhibition, appeared in the February 1974 issue of *Craft Horizons.*

To a Slave Named Job. "Job's Cigar Store Indian," in polychromed wood, is believed to have been made by a slave (c. 1825) for a tobacconist in Freehold, New Jersey.

Sacred to the Memory. Based on an unsigned watercolor, "Mourning Picture for Polly Botsford and Her Children," painted c. 1813 and found in Connecticut.

239

Trompe l'Oeil. Several nineteenth-century country artisans became masters of illusion, developing techniques that enabled them to simulate, on ordinary pine, the inlays, veneers, and graining of expensive furniture.

A Blessing of Women. I owe a special debt of gratitude to Jean Lipman and Alice Winchester, who organized the Whitney exhibition and made a superb book out of it, for much of the biographical information incorporated into this poem.

Page 16. *The Crystal Cage*. Contributed, together with an original collage, to Dore Ashton's *A Joseph Cornell Album* (The Viking Press, 1974). My title is taken from an early work by the late maker of magical boxes.

Page 18. *Signs and Portents*. Since this poem was written in 1976–1977, Ramses II has been returned to Egypt from Paris after treatment for his infection; the delicate operation of removing the Caryatids from the Erectheum is progressing slowly; the Caves of Lascaux have been reopened to visitors on a limited basis; no further information has reached me from Saint Helena about the fate of Jonathan the giant tortoise.

Page 22. *The Lincoln Relics*. The exhibition of Lincoln relics was held at the Library of Congress during the term of my appointment as Consultant in Poetry. My only previous experience of living in Washington had been during World War II, when I was in military service.

Page 26. *Meditations on Death*. "La Morte Meditata." My original version of Ungaretti's hermetic poem, which I called "Death Thoughts," was written during his triumphal visit to the United States in the spring of 1970. By invitation of The Academy of American Poets, Ungaretti's American translators participated in his reading at the Guggenheim Museum in New York. Ungaretti died on June 1, 1970, shortly after his return to Italy.

Page 49. *Around Pastor Bonhoeffer*. Dietrich Bonhoeffer was a German Lutheran pastor and theologian whose Christian conscience forced him, against the pacific temper of his spirit, to accept the necessity of political activism and to join in a conspiracy for the murder of Hitler. The plot failed, and he was arrested by the Gestapo (1943).

On April 9, 1945, he was hanged at Flossenburg extermination camp. His brother Klaus and two brothers-in-law were also destroyed. Some of the details of the poem have their source in Bonhoeffer's two posthumous publications, *The Cost of Discipleship* and *Letters and Papers from Prison,* and in the biography by his disciple Eberhard Bethge.

Page 52. *King of the River.* Within two weeks after leaving the ocean to swim up the rivers of the Northwest and spawn, the bounding Pacific salmon degenerates into "an aged, colorless, and almost lifeless fish." The same geriatric process in humans takes some twenty to forty years.

Page 59. *Summer Solstice.* I am indebted to Andrew Field for helping me construe the Russian of this early lyric by Mandelstam.

Page 60. *Tristia.* Mandelstam's Latin title, meaning Poems of Sorrow, alludes to the elegiac epistles of Ovid, which the Roman poet began on his journey into exile in Tomis. Ovid spoke of the sorrow of exile, of his unconquerable will to survive and to write, of his loves, and of his hope that he might be allowed to return to Rome. Mandelstam never returned from the prison camp to which Stalin sent him.

Page 70. *Hand-rolled Cigarettes.* Devotees of the hand-rolled cigarette in Russia are said to be divided into opposite camps, according to their preference for rolling their tobacco in *Pravda* or *Izvestia,* the two top official newspapers. One of the jokes heard in Moscow literary circles has to do with a man who is sent to jail for a political crime. As soon as he is put behind bars, he is surrounded by prisoners who are eager for information about the outside world. "What's the news?" they inquire. "How should I know?" he replies, with a shrug. "I don't smoke."

Yevtushenko's poem is full of political allusions, beginning, in the second stanza, with Stalin's infamous fantasy of a Doctors' Plot. The last line of the poem parodies a celebrated boast by Khrushchev.

Page 74. *The Gladiators.* The impulsive monk who tried to stop the bloodshed suffered his martyrdom at the hands of the enraged spectators about A.D. 400. The scandal of his dismemberment led to the proscription of man-to-man combats. In actual historical sequence, which I have telescoped, the barbarous Children's Crusades did not eventuate till the thirteenth century.

Page 76. *Bolsheviks*. Aba Stolzenberg (1905-1941) was an obscure Yiddish poet who came to the United States from Poland. Irving Howe, in the course of compiling *A Treasury of Yiddish Poetry* (Holt, Rinehart & Winston) in collaboration with Eliezer Greenberg, introduced me to Stolzenberg's work and assisted me with the text.

Page 77. *The Mound Builders*. The civilization of the Mound Builders, of whom regrettably little is known, flourished between A.D. 900 and 1100. The site of their community in Georgia was later held sacred by the Creek Nation. At the time of my visit to the Ocmulgee National Monument, in the spring of 1962, President Kennedy had just announced the resumption of nuclear testing by the United States.

Pages 80–83. *Boris Pasternak; Dante; Cleopatra*. Anna Akhmatova (1888-1966), friend and peer of Pasternak, is one of the great figures of modern Russian poetry. Max Hayward and I worked in close collaboration for several years on *Poems of Akhmatova* (Atlantic–Little, Brown, 1973).

Page 84. *The Artist*. Written following the suicide in New York of my friend the painter Mark Rothko, on February 25, 1970.

Page 85. *The Bottom of the Glass*. This poem is modeled on some untitled lines by the contemporary Russian poet Naum Korzhavin, a number of whose poems I translated for *Pages from Tarusa: New Voices in Russian Writing* (Little, Brown), edited by Andrew Field. Korzhavin (born Mandel) is now living in the United States.

Page 89. *The Testing-Tree*. When I was a boy in Worcester, Massachusetts, my family lived on top of a hill, at the thin edge of the city, with the woods beyond. Much of the time I was alone, but I learned how not to be lonely, exploring the surrounding fields and the old Indian trails. In the games that I improvised, most of them involved with running, climbing, and a variety of ball-skills, I was a fierce competitor, representing in turn myself and my imaginary opponent. It did not occur to me to be surprised that "I" was always the winner.

The stone-throwing that figures in the poem was of a somewhat special order, since it did more than try my skill: it challenged destiny. My life hinged on the three throws permitted me, according to my rules. If I hit the target-oak once, somebody would love me; if I hit it twice, I should be a poet; if I scored all three times, I should never die. A friend of mine tells me that what I have recorded here is recognizable as an ancient ritual, and that the patriarchal scarred oak, as I have described it, is transparently a manifestation of the King of the Wood. Such mysteries for a Worcester childhood!

Page 116. *The Thief.* "Mamertine blood" alludes to the Mamertine Prison in the Roman Forum, which has a dungeon reputed to have been occupied by St. Peter. The "baldpate [who] awaits his rhetorical cue" behind the balcony is my image for Mussolini.

Page 157. *Father and Son.* The Gemara is the section of commentary in the Talmud on the oral law of the Jews.

Page 162. *The Last Picnic.* Written following the bombing of Pearl Harbor, December 7, 1941.

Page 172. *The Daughters of the Horseleech.* "The horseleach hath two daughters, crying, Give, give." — Proverbs 30:15.

Page 183. *The Reckoning.* Original title, "What Have You Done?"

Page 190. *For the Word Is Flesh.* Lessius and Tolet (third stanza) came to me by way of Burton's *Anatomy of Melancholy,* a book that I discovered at college and that I still consult with undiminished pleasure. Leonhard Lessius, a contemporary of Burton's, was a Flemish theologian and Jesuit. Franciscus Tolet, a sixteenth-century Spanish churchman and scholar, wrote an obscure commentary on Aristotle. The source of my information about "fantasies of Er" was Plato's *Republic,* Book X. Er, the son of Armenius, returned to earth after being slain in battle and gave a vivid report on the migrations and destinies of souls in the other world. As for the hypothetical "Florentine" and his deathbed revisions (concluding stanza), he was, in all probability, suggested by an account I read of Proust's last day. Proust was said to have asked his servant to bring him a certain page wherein Bergotte is portrayed in the agony of death — because "I have several retouchings to make here, now that I find myself in the same predicament."

Page 205. *The Pivot*. Original title, "Soul's Adventure."

Page 223. *Transformations*. Original title, "Elemental Metamorphosis."

Page 231. *The Separation*. Original title, "Who Tears the Serpent from the Flesh."

INDEX

A BLESSING OF WOMEN, 12
A CHOICE OF WEAPONS, 141
A leopard no more secret, 214
A man with a leaf in his head, 55
A roaring company that festive
    night, 114
A SPARK OF LAUREL, 146
A sweet, a delicate white mouse, 103
AFTER THE LAST DYNASTY, 62
AGAIN! AGAIN! 88
"Again I come to buy the image
    fated," 181
All night he ran, his body air, 223
AMBERGRIS, 203
Amid that Platonic statuary, of
    athletes, 138
AMONG THE GODS, 101
An agitation of the air, 119
AN OLD CRACKED TUNE, 87
And everywhere, all over, men have
    sighed, 221
APPROACH OF AUTUMN, 204
AROUND PASTOR BONHOEFFER, 49
AS FLOWERS ARE, 102
As flowers have wars that the
    philosophic eye, 102
As if I were composed of dust and
    air, 233
At breakfast mother sipped her
    buttermilk, 66
At his incipient sun, 224

Before I am completely shriven, 193
BENEDICTION, 229
BETWEEN THE ACTS, 173

BEYOND REASON, 235
Bless Zeruah Higley Guernsey, 12
BOLSHEVIKS (STOLZENBERG), 76
BORIS PASTERNAK (AKHMATOVA), 80
Brain, be ice, 202
BY LAMPLIGHT, 128

CARELESS LOVE, 170
CHANGE, 187
CLEOPATRA (AKHMATOVA), 83
Cold-eyed, in Naples once, 22
Come sit beneath the tariff walls, 167
Concentrical, the universe and I, 188
CONFIDENTIAL INSTRUCTIONS, 166
Conjugations of the verb "to be," 21
Considered by the logical brief clock,
    197

DANTE (AKHMATOVA), 82
Darling, darling, by narrow
    ambages, 210
DEATH IN MOONLIGHT, 214
DECIDUOUS BRANCH, 200
Declines at evening from your eyes,
    195
Dissolving in the chemic vat, 187
Dreaming of Africa, 8

EAGLE, 226
Earth was my home, but even there
    I was a stranger, 48
Echo, the beating of the tide, 209
END OF SUMMER, 119
Endlessly to no end wending, 222
Even after his death he did not
    return, 82

Fallen, so freshly fallen, 122
Fate hired me once to play a villain's
 part, 173
FATHER AND SON, 157
FIRESTICKS, 21
FIRST LOVE, 224
FOR PROSERPINE, 216
For the sake of the record, 72
FOR THE WORD IS FLESH, 190
FOREIGN AFFAIRS, 108
Forget the tube of bark, 207

GEOMETRY OF MOODS, 188
GIRL WITH SAMPLER, 10
God banish from your house, 229
GOOSE POND, 120
Goose Pond's imaginable snows, 120
GRAMMAR LESSON, 105
GREEN WAYS, 99

HAND-ROLLED CIGARETTES
 (YEVTUSHENKO), 70
Have you any old clothes to sell? 168
HE, 206
He heard the centuries tick slowly,
 205
He runs before the wise men: he, 206
He who has compared himself to the
 eye of a horse, 80
Her grace is not of any part, 110
HERMETIC POEM, 132
His paintings grew darker every
 year, 84
HOW LONG IS THE NIGHT? 179
How much I disapprove of it! 143
How shall I keep this violence in,
 131

I abdicate my daily self that bled, 236
I DREAMED THAT I WAS OLD, 220
I dreamed that I was old: in stale
 declension, 220
I have walked through many lives,
 35
I made myself an expert in farewells,
 60
I said to the watcher at the gate, 156
I touch you in the night, whose gift
 was you, 97
I wait. I deepen in the room, 192

I was fishing in the abandoned
 reservoir, 4
If, in a fisherman's hut, you poke, 70
If the water were clear enough, 52
Ignorance, error, cupidity, and sin,
 133
In a Roman tram, where the famous
 Roman mob, 116
IN A STRANGE HOUSE, 232
In that hotel near my life, 45
In the zero of the night, in the
 lipping hour, 112
INDIAN SUMMER AT LAND'S END, 58
Inside, a hundred doors by which to
 leave, 165
INVOCATION, 176
It darted across the pond, 15
It was the dingiest bird, 56
Its narrow head that gnaws the
 breast, 231
I've tried to seal it in, 1

Jittery, missing their cues, 49
Jonathan, the last of the giant
 tortoises, 18
JOURNAL FOR MY DAUGHTER, 39
Just who was so powerful and
 clever? 6

KING OF THE RIVER, 52

LAST WORDS, 225
Let me not say it, let me not reveal,
 99
Let the old geezers jig on Penn-, 77
Let's spin the bottle, 93
Listen: from sleep's long pillow I
 arise, 225
Love knocked again at my door, 88
LOVERS RELENTLESSLY, 212
Lovers relentlessly contend to be,
 212

MASTER AND MISTRESS, 233
ME AND THE ROCK, 222
MEDITATIONS ON DEATH (UNGARETTI),
 26
MENS CREATRIX, 202
Mother was a crack of light, 47
MOTION OF WISH, 227

Mourn for Polly Botsford, aged
  thirty-nine, 9
My architects, forsaking me, 174
My heart felt need to die, 129
My mother never forgave my father,
  86
My name is sand: I make, 175
My name is Solomon Levi, 87
MY SISTERS, 32
MY SURGEONS, 153
My surgeons are a savage band, 153

NIGHT LETTER, 160
NIGHT-PIECE, 221
NO WORD, 177
Not by planning and not by
  choosing, 85
Now in the suburbs and the falling
  light, 157
O Heart: this is a dream I had, or
  not a dream, 198
O ruined father dead, long sweetly
  rotten, 190
O sister of the shadow, 26
OFF POINT LOTUS, 130
Oh the good times! the laughter on
  the hill! 178
On my way home from school, 89
On the anvil of love my flesh has
  been hammered out, 179
One summer, like a stone, 2
Only, when I am sudden loss, 196
OPEN THE GATES, 184
ORGANIC BLOOM, 234
Orioles live in the elms, and in
  classical verse, 59
Our purple tongues that testify, 216

PARTICULAR LULLABY, 195
PARTING, 219
Parting, I take with me completed
  June, 219
Pigeon, who are to me, 183
POEM, 198
Poor john, who joined in make of
  wrong, 159
POSTSCRIPT, 210
PROMISE ME, 196
PROPHECY ON LETHE, 209

QUINNAPOXET, 4

Reading in Li Po, 62
REFLECTION BY A MAILBOX, 151
REGARD OF TANGENTS, 215
Reviewing me without undue
  elation, 141
REVOLVING MEDITATION, 143
RIVER ROAD, 64
ROBIN REDBREAST, 56
ROUTE SIX, 33
ROVER, 131

SACRED TO THE MEMORY, 9
Say to me only, 104
She had already kissed Antony's dead
  lips, 83
She sat by the window, 10
SHE WEPT, SHE RAILED, 107
She wept, she railed, she spurned the
  meat, 107
SIGNS AND PORTENTS, 18
SILENCE (AKHMADULINA), 6
SINGLE VISION, 193
SO INTRICATELY IS THIS WORLD
  RESOLVED, 228
So intricately is this world resolved,
  228
SOTTO VOCE, 104
Soul of my soul, in the ancestral
  wood, 176
STRANGE CALENDAR, 197
SUMMER SOLSTICE (MANDELSTAM), 59

Taking infection from the vulgar air,
  201
That pack of scoundrels, 69
That year of the cloud, when my
  marriage failed, 64
THE APPROACH TO THEBES, 112
THE ARTIST, 84
The blessing in this conscious fruit,
  the hurt, 235
THE BOTTOM OF THE GLASS, 85
The brain constructs its systems to
  enclose, 234
THE CATCH, 15
The city squats on my back, 33
THE CLASS WILL COME TO ORDER, 138

THE CRYSTAL CAGE, 16
THE CUSTOMS COLLECTOR'S REPORT, 72
THE DARK AND THE FAIR, 114
THE DAUGHTERS OF THE HORSELEECH, 172
The daughters of the horseleech crying "Give! Give!" 172
THE DRAGONFLY, 122
The dwindling pole, 226
The early violets we saw together, 204
THE ECONOMIST'S SONG, 167
THE FITTING OF THE MASK, 181
The flesh has knowledge of the flesh, 215
THE FLIGHT OF APOLLO, 48
THE GAME, 93
THE GLADIATORS, 74
The guests in their summer colors have fled, 162
THE GUILTY MAN, 180
THE HARSH JUDGEMENT, 165
THE HEMORRHAGE, 163
THE ILLUMINATION, 45
THE ILLUSIONIST, 175
The intellectuals at the feast, 171
THE KNOT, 1
THE LAST PICNIC, 162
THE LAST QUESTION, 178
THE LAYERS, 35
THE LINCOLN RELICS, 22
THE MAGIC CURTAIN, 66
THE MAN UPSTAIRS, 111
The man who sold his lawn to standard oil, 125
The memory of time is here imprisoned, 232
THE MOUND BUILDERS, 77
THE MULCH, 55
THE OLD CLOTHES MAN, 168
The old man sick with boyhood fears, 111
The people made a ring, 163
THE PIVOT, 205
THE PORTRAIT, 86
THE QUARREL, 30
THE RECKONING, 183
THE SCIENCE OF THE NIGHT, 97
THE SCOURGE, 129

The season stalls, unseasonably fair, 58
The secret my heart keeps, 132
THE SEPARATION, 231
THE SIGNAL FROM THE HOUSE, 156
THE SUMMING-UP, 140
THE SUPPER BEFORE LAST, 171
THE SYSTEM, 69
THE TESTING-TREE, 89
THE THIEF, 116
THE THING THAT EATS THE HEART, 127
The thing that eats the heart comes wild with years, 127
THE TUTORED CHILD, 155
THE UNQUIET ONES, 31
THE UNWITHERED GARLAND, 110
The urgent letter that I try to write, 160
THE WALTZER IN THE HOUSE, 103
THE WAR AGAINST THE TREES, 125
THE WAY DOWN, 135
The word I spoke in anger, 30
THE WORDS OF THE PREACHER, 201
The years of my life were odd that now are even, 180
They came on ponies, barefoot, 76
They fought in heavy armor, 74
This body, tapped of every drop of breath, 203
THIS DAY THIS WORLD, 174
This man, this poet, said, 146
THREE FLOORS, 47
Three years I lolled in that country of the girls, 130
Through evolutions of the seed, 227
Through portal and through peristyle, 177
Time swings her burning hands, 135
TO A SLAVE NAMED JOB, 8
To climb the belltower, 16
TO THE READER (BAUDELAIRE), 133
TRANSFORMATIONS, 223
TRISTIA (MANDELSTAM), 60
TROMPE L'OEIL, 11
TWILIGHT, 192

VERY TREE, 207
VITA NUOVA, 236

Waking was laughing then, 105
We are two countries girded for the war, 108
Welcome, eccentric life, 128
WELCOME THE WRATH, 159
WHAT OF THE NIGHT? 2
When I stand in the center of that man's madness, 151
When, on your dangerous mission gone, 166
WHEN THE DEAD ARISE, 218
When the dead arise, 218
WHEN THE LIGHT FALLS, 100
When the light falls, it falls on her, 100
When young I scribbled, boasting, on my wall, 140

Who have been lonely once, 170
Who whispered, *Souls have shapes?* 32
Whoever made this piece began, 11
Winter, that coils in the thickets now, 200
Within the city of the burning cloud, 184
Within the grated dungeon of the eye, 101
WORDS FOR THE UNKNOWN MAKERS: A GARLAND OF COMMEMORATIVE VERSES, 8

Years ago I lost, 31
Your mother, whom the mirror-world has claimed, 155
Your turn, Grass of confusion, 39